YOU AND I

A COMEDY IN THREE ACTS

BY

PHILIP BARRY

NEW YORK
SAMUEL FRENCH
PUBLISHER
25 WEST 45TH STREET

LONDON
SAMUEL FRENCH, LTD.
26 SOUTHAMPTON STREET
STRAND

"You and I"

Printed in the United States of America by
THE RICHMOND HILL RECORD, RICHMOND HILL, N. Y.

To

E. S. B.

MY FAVORITE PERSON

FOR HIS FRIENDSHIP, ENCOURAGEMENT AND INVALUABLE INSTRUCTION, MY DEBT TO PROFESSOR GEORGE P. BAKER IS, AND WILL REMAIN, BEYOND MEASURE.

P. B.

"You and I," produced by Richard G. Herndon and directed by Robert Milton, was first presented in New York at the Belmont Theater on February 19th, 1923, with the following cast:

MAITLAND WHITE .... *H. B. Warner*
NANCY WHITE .... *Lucile Watson*
RODERICK WHITE .... *Geoffrey Kerr*
VERONICA DUANE .... *Frieda Inescort*
GEOFFREY NICHOLS .... *Reginald Mason*
G. T. WARREN .... *Ferdinand Gottschalk*
ETTA .... *Beatrice Miles*

The setting for Act I was designed by Raymond Sovey; for Act II by J. L. Shute and Robert Goode, of The 47 Workshop, Harvard University.

CHARACTERS
(In the order of their appearance)

VERONICA DUANE
RODERICK WHITE
NANCY WHITE
MAITLAND WHITE
ETTA
G. T. WARREN
GEOFFREY NICHOLS

SCENES

ACT I.
The library of the Whites' country home in Mount Kisco, Westchester County, New York. A late September evening.

ACT II.
"The Studio" in the attic, an afternoon the following May.

ACT III.
"The Studio," later the same evening.

YOU AND I

ACT I

Here you are, in the library of the Whites' country home in Mount Kisco, Westchester County, New York.

The Whites' home is one of those rambling white houses that began as a farmhouse and has been added to year by year as the family grew, and the family's fortunes prospered. In architecture, it is nearer Colonial than anything else. There was always plenty of land, but the orchard, of which MAITLAND WHITE *is so proud, he planted himself.*

When you come for your first week-end, he will delight in telling you that when NANCY *and he bought the place, twenty years ago, the room in which you now stand was, with the exception of a tiny kitchen, the entire lower floor. The second beam from the left in the ceiling will show you where the partition came between living and dining rooms.*

The big hall by which you entered is the west wing—that came first—and the spacious dining room and study are the east wing, which was built four years later. The servants' wing was added at the same time. The little cottage down by the swimming-pool is of course quite new. That is to be JEAN'S, *when she grows up and is ready to be married—fancy* JEANIE *married!*

You will be awfully surprised and say What! —this enormous place grown out of a little old farmhouse? And MAITLAND *will chuckle and say Oh, Nanny and I have had no end of fun out of it, haven't we, Nanny? And like as not, the next time you come (as you will, if they like you) he will begin to tell you about it all over again. But* NANCY *will stop him, without in the least hurting his feelings.*

The library—which is also the main living-room—is a huge, uneven, motherly sort of a room that pats your hand as you come into it, and tells you to sit down and be comfortable with the rest of us. Out here we don't even know that there is *such a place as the City!*

There is a large white fireplace, with two ample chairs flanking it. A long table stands just away from the center of the room. There are a few more easy-chairs, and a writing-desk. A great sofa invites you to abandon yourself to its lethal depths. Wherever there is not a window or a door, there are built-in bookcases, filled with books. MAITLAND *will show you, among the really fine etchings upon the wall, two rare Whistlers, in which he takes a just pride. You enter—through glass doors at the right—a kind of sun-room, from which, if you are sufficiently enterprising, you may proceed through the garden into the orchard. The woodwork of the library is a soft ivory. There is no scheme of decoration, but the whole effect is one of warmth and light and color. It is what you would call, not a beautiful, but a charming room.*

The time is about seven o'clock of a late September evening, and someone, someone whom you must wait a moment to see, is playing a frivolous tune on the piano in the sun-

room. In the middle of a measure, the music stops abruptly. There is a short silence, followed by the bang of a discord. Then, with her head high, thoroughly angry, VERONICA DUANE *enters and traverses the library, nearly to the hall.*

She is about nineteen, slim, of medium height, with a decidedly pretty, high-bred face, lovely hair, lovely hands, and a soft, low-pitched voice—whatever she may be saying. Heredity, careful upbringing, education and travel have combined to invest her with a poise far in advance of her years. She has attained the impossible—complete sophistication without the loss of bloom. Her self-confidence is, you will be happy to know, free from any taint of youthful cock-sureness.

RONNY *(as she is fortunately called) was made to wear clothes well, and she wears her present out-of-door ones superlatively so. There is something in the ensemble—it may be a scarf, the marking of a sweater, or the tongue of a shoe—that everyone will have next summer:* RONNY *adopted it at Deauville last Spring.*

Following her comes RODERICK WHITE, *with the fireplace as his objective. There he stands leaning back against a chair, stuffing a pipe with tobacco and looking just a little bit scared.*

He is a well-set-up, thoroughly nice boy about twenty-one, with high color, hair carefully brushed, a disarming smile. Although his expression is bright and animated, his countenance appears to be totally without guile. Only RICKY *knows the multitude of scrapes that he has got him out of.*

If you come near enough, particularly on a rainy day, you will catch, as it hovers about his golf clothes, a thoroughly satisfactory aroma of peat-smoke. RICKY *has a proper regard for old clo'. His polo-shirt, though it may be a little frayed, has the merit of being clean. His brown-and-white shoes—genuine antiques—have not.*

RONNY. *(With a rigid back to him)* I think I'll be—going home.

RICKY. *(Amiability itself)* Good idea—if you expect to dress and be back here in time for dinner. *(A pause.)* Well—you needn't be so darn snootey about it. (RONNY *wheels about and faces him.)*

RONNY. Ricky—I could kill you for doing that.

RICKY. *(Puffing on his pipe)* I've been resisting the impulse all summer—and when you turned your head and looked up that way—well, it was rather pleasant.

RONNY. I don't see how you dared!

RICKY. Oh, come on, Ronny—you can't get away with that. You loved it.

RONNY. Who said I didn't! For months you've had me literally quaking in my boots. Because I knew that if ever you did, I'd—I'd——

RICKY. *(Bearing in her direction)* Ronny! Did you know that, too . . . *(She nods her head, dumbly.)* And *do* you now—as much as I do . . . ?

RONNY. Hang it—of course I do! On the fifteenth of October you're going abroad for three years. For the love of Pete, why couldn't you have held out just two weeks more? Then you'd have gone, and I'd have forgotten you. And that would have been all there was to it.

RICKY. In a pig's eye.

RONNY. I tell you it would! And now—after this—— *(She flings a magazine from table to sofa.)* Oh—a sweet winter I'll put in, getting over you!

RICKY. *(Genuinely dismayed)* Getting *over* me? Gosh, I don't want you to do *that!*

RONNY. No—I'll sit around doing basket-work, while you and your little playmates at the Beaux-Arts scamper up and down Paris.

RICKY. *(Grandly)* I am going abroad to study architecture—not to go on parties.

RONNY. Show *me* a student on the Left Bank who doesn't study life! Thanks, Rick. By Spring you will be but a memory.

RICKY. But—but Ronny—can't you get it into your silly head that I'm *really* in love with you? I'm—you've—oh, damn it—*won't* you marry me?

(RONNY'S *hand, in a quick gesture, covers his. For one breathless moment their eyes hold them together.)*

RONNY. Ricky! *(Then she removes her hand, and shakes her head with conviction.)* Uh-uh. It's awfully nice of you—but I couldn't wait three years for the Prince of Wales.

RICKY. *(Moodily)* Fat lot you love me.

RONNY. Oh—don't think I'm an absolute dud—*(With a trace of embarrassment)* You—know how it is—with Father and Mother, don't you?

RICKY. Why—they don't hit it off too well, do they?

RONNY. Mother's never said a word to me—but of course she's simply sticking it out till I'm what they call "settled." I had it all planned to marry the next person I was honestly fond of. But now you—you egg—you've ruined it. I'll have to forget *you* first. It would be such a filthy trick—when I—when there was someone I actually—— *(She shudders.)* Oh—I couldn't stand it!

RICKY. I can't imagine being—to anyone but you, really I can't.

RONNY. *(Softly)* It would be too delightful, to be—to you. *(There is a pause.)*

RICKY. *(A sudden idea)* Listen, Ronny: there's no reason why we *shouldn't* be—I'll go into Father's factory, instead. Mr. Warren said he'd start me at two thousand a year, and if I was any good——

RONNY. But Rick—you've *always* meant to be an architect. I won't have you wash out on it for me.

RICKY. Oh—will you listen?—I'm not washing out on anything. I'll study on the side—and drift into it gradually. I can go to night school——

RONNY. "'Whom are you?' said Cyril."

RICKY. But why not? Other people have. Life shouldn't be all gravy, anyway. After ten years of school and college I feel like a burglar at the prospect of riding Dad for three years more. I know I could swing it every bit as well, right here on my own.

RONNY. But that sounds like such a makeshift. And supposing once you got into business you had to stay put?

RICKY. Well, that's no calamity. Father dished painting in order to marry Nanny. And do you suppose he's ever regretted it? Look at them!

RONNY. I know—they're so happy, it's painful. But——

RICKY. Ronny, it's simply that I want *you*—so much more than anything else, that it's silly even to talk about it.

RONNY. Are you sure you'll keep *on* wanting me more?

RICKY. Damn right, I will!

RONNY. *(Thoughtfully)* There's a kink in it somewhere. . . .

RICKY. Oh—you're full of cold tea. Listen: I'll work like the very devil, and next summer we'll be married. What do you say?

RONNY. *(After a troubled pause)* Why—I've no really strong objections. . . .

RICKY. *(In embarrassed delight)* Oh, Lord—this is wonderful. . . . *(She rises and faces him. They stand looking at each other, silently.* RICKY *finally ventures it.)* Dearest. . . .

RONNY. Angel. . . .

RICKY. Darling. . . .

RONNY. Lover. . . .

RICKY. *(Groping for it)* Uh—uh—*Precious.*

RONNY. *(Dramatically)* My tr-r-r-easure. *(He presents a cheek, but* RONNY *edges away.)* Not on your life. . . . (RICKY *intrepidly kisses her on the cheek. She laughs.)* Gosh, Rick—you're poor!

RICKY. How do you know?

RONNY. I read a book. *(At which* RICKY *takes her in his arms, as if she were made of spun glass.)*

RICKY. "To Veronica from Roderick, with love." *(He kisses her lightly, but unmistakably.)*

RONNY. *(Softly)* Oh—how diverting.

RICKY. I'm going to tell Mother!

RONNY. *(In consternation)* She'll crown me!

RICKY. Rot, my child. She'll think what a clever lad her son is.

RONNY. I'm scared of her. . . .

RICKY. *(Pooh-poohing)* Scared of Nanny?—Why, she's nothing but a kid.

RONNY. She appals me. She knows so much. . .

RICKY. She'll be all for it. Just you see—— *(He starts toward the door, but comes back.)* Ronny—honestly—I simply adore you. . . .

RONNY. *(With a faint smile)* Dear—you've got nothing on me. *(On this second expedition he reaches the door, and calls upstairs.)*

RICKY. Mother! *(Where can she be?)* Dearest! *(Can she have gone out?)* Ho, Nanny—stick out your neck!

NANCY. *(An enchanting voice from above)* What is it, you simpleton?

RICKY. What do you think?

NANCY. I think it's time you changed for dinner.

RICKY. Ronny and I are engaged. Can you beat it?

NANCY. Wh-a-a-t—?

RICKY. We have plighted our troth. Big news. C'mon down! *(He returns to* RONNY.) Beau'ful—I feel awfully sacred all of a sudden. Tell you what I'll do; I'll go to church with you in the morning.

RONNY. Check. The Maiden's Prayer.

RICKY. Then I'll take you on for nine fast holes before luncheon. Give you a stroke a hole—two, on the sixth—and beat the shoes off you!

RONNY. You lie, Dumbell, you won't.

RICKY. A dollar a hole. Are you on?

RONNY. *(Scornfully)* Am I on! For nine dollars, I'd——

(NANCY WHITE *appears in the hall doorway, carrying a half-written letter in her hand. She is a young forty, not so short, not so tall, but anyway with a slim, girlish figure, lively, humorous brown eyes, dark brown hair, and a manner as charming as her appearance. Despite her poise, one feels that her age is merely put on—youth dwells in her spirit, and no mere calendar can oust it.* RICKY *meets her at the door, and they enter together, his arm about her shoulder.)*

RICKY. *(With a gesture toward* RONNY) Behold!—My willing slave.

NANCY. *(A brave attempt at severity)* Veronica—is what Roderick tells me true?

RONNY. All but the "slave," Mrs. White.

(NANCY *looks from one to the other, goes to* RONNY, *takes her hand, gazes into her eyes for a moment, and then kisses her on the cheek.)*

NANCY. *(Emotionally)* My dear! *(She brushes away a hypothetical tear, and reaches one hand out behind her, to* RICKY) My first-born child!

RICKY. *(For* RONNY'S *information)* Nanny wanted to go on the stage once. She just eats a thing like this.

NANCY. *(Pointing an imperious finger toward the sofa)* Ricky—sit down there! (RICKY *obeys, grinning.* NANCY *designates a place beside him.)* Veronica—— (RONNY *sits at his side, a little frightened.* NANCY *pulls a large chair around, and sits facing them.)* Now, you two precious idiots, we'll talk this over.

RICKY. *(To* RONNY) Isn't she immense? *(He affects a most solemn expression, and leans forward attentively, resting his chin upon his hand.)*

NANCY. I thought the fact of your living next door to each other for twelve summers would act as an anti-toxin.

RONNY. You could have knocked me over with a feather, Mrs. White.

NANCY. I dare say. But of course it's quite out of the question. You're nothing but children.

RICKY. *(Shaking his head reprovingly)* Gosh, Nanny—that's awfully old stuff. . . .

NANCY. *(With some acerbity)* Roderick—be kind enough to reserve your infantile comments. (RICKY *subsides. She leans back with sigh.)* Nothing but children. It is beautiful, my dears, but quite, quite ridiculous.

RICKY. Pardon the interruption,—but how old were you when *you* became a Married Maiden?

NANCY. That has nothing to do with it!

RICKY. *(Indulgently)* I know—but just as a matter of record. . . .

NANCY. *(The dignified mother of two children)* I was—nineteen. But——

RICKY. You mean a couple of weeks past eighteen. What're you, Ronny?

RONNY. I'll be twenty in December. Big girl.

RICKY. Check. And how about Dad?

NANCY. He was a great deal older than you are!

RICKY. Your memory's failing! He had me just four months.

NANCY. *(Ironically)* I don't want to be sordid—but what *do* you expect to live on?

RICKY. Query: What did *you* live on, Darling?

NANCY. Why—I had a little of my own, and your father worked.

RICKY. *(With a gesture)* 'S a perfect equation!

RONNY. I've about two thousand a year from Aunt Isabel's estate. Dad's promised me a house.

NANCY. *(To* RICKY*)* And may I ask what you intend doing about your architecture?

RONNY. *(Leaning forward)* You and me both, Mrs. White. . . .

RICKY. Quiet, Child—let me manage this. I'm going like a breeze. *(To* NANCY*)* Well, you see, I'm going to pass that up, and——

NANCY. *(Really troubled)* But——

RICKY. Oh—maybe not for good. Maybe, by and by, when we get on our feet——

NANCY. "By and by!" Somehow, that sounds vaguely reminiscent to me. Unless you do it now, you'll never do it!—That's certain as death and my hay-fever.

RICKY. Well, really—what if I don't? I mean, you told me that father wanted to paint, or something—but you and he were married at twenty-one and eighteen respectively, and he went into business, and stayed there. What I mean is, it seems to me that you two have made a pretty good go of it.

NANCY. *(Proudly)* We have made an uncommonly good go of it. But—— *(She scrutinizes* RICKY'S *ankles in despair.)* Oh—your stockings again! Ronny—can't *you* make him wear garters?

RONNY. Isn't it awful?—Slippety-slop. . . .

NANCY. What you find attractive in him, I'm sure I can't see.—I was saying . . . ? Ah, yes—my reminiscences—— *(She hesitates. Then to* RONNY*)* Of course, you look very charming as you are. But we dine at a quarter before eight. . . . (RONNY *rises and moves toward the hall.)*

RONNY. Then I'd better shove off.

NANCY. *(Just as she is about to go out)* Oh—uh—Veronica——

RONNY. *(Turning)* Yes . . . ?

NANCY. Do you think you really love my Ricky? *(A short pause.* RONNY *looks straight at* NANCY.)

RONNY. *(Simply)* I've—never given a happy hang for anyone else. I'd—simply—lie down and die for him.

(RICKY *rises and makes for her, but a sweep of* NANCY'S *arm intercepts him.)*

NANCY. A quarter before eight. And—I think it will be all right—somehow——

RONNY. Oh—you *are* a dear. . . .

RICKY. *(Calling after her)* Make it seven-thirty, if you can. President of Dad's company's coming, and we may rate a cocktail!

RONNY. *(A voice from the hall)* Right-o!

(NANCY *goes to the desk, with her unfinished letter.)*

NANCY. I'm writing to your sister. Your love?

RICKY. Sure. But don't say anything about Ronny and I——

NANCY. *(Automatically)* "—about Ronny and *me.*"

RICKY. *(Grammar is an affectation)* —about Ronny and I. You know Jean—she'd have it all over the school in six minutes.

NANCY. Now—I want to talk to you sensibly.

RICKY. Shoot, Darling——

(NANCY *opens a drawer of the desk. It is filled to overflowing with small pieces of paper. Two fall upon the floor.* RICKY *picks them up and looks at them.)*

NANCY. You see these?

RICKY. Sketches!—Father's . . . ?

NANCY. Yes. Before I give Roberts his clothes to press, I always go through the pockets. Not more than twenty times in twenty years have I failed to find one or two of these, all nicely folded up and tucked away. He does murals, too. That's why the wall beside the telephone is repapered so often. . . . *(Looking at sketches, which* RICKY *gives her.)* Charming, aren't they . . . ? *(She puts them back and closes the drawer. Taking* RICKY'S *arm, they return together to the sofa.)*

RICKY. But what's Dad's foolishness got to do with my——?

NANCY. There's something very sad in that folly, Rick. It's like the beating of clipped wings . . . longing for flight. . . . (RICKY *stares at her.)*

RICKY. *(Disgustedly)* Oh—if you're going to get deep on me——

NANCY. You've no idea how deep it goes. . . . *(She studies his face for a moment and then continues, matter-of-factly)* Now, Ronny is a sweet, lovable girl. And if the truth must be known, I heartily approve of early marriages, when—— (RICKY *leans over and pecks her cheek.)*

RICKY. Great!

NANCY. Behave yourself, and listen to me!—*When* they are possible without too great sacrifices. Ricky—from the time you began to play with blocks, you've wanted to study architecture. Don't you still . . . ?

RICKY. Why, of course I do. But I can't have both—and I want Ronny more.

NANCY. We might arrange——

RICKY. To carry the two of us? That's like you, dear—but no, thanks. When I'm married, I've got to be on my own. Maybe I'm in the same place Father was. Well—I know what I want most, just the way he did. It's a simple question of values.

NANCY. Your values may shift a little, later on.

RICKY. *(By way of refutation)* Did Father's?

NANCY. And when you're forty or so, you may look on love as a kind of captivating robber—who chatted so sweetly, as he plucked your destiny out of your pocket. . . .

RICKY. There you go again! Ask Dad—*he* knows!

(From the hall is heard a whistled refrain which, possibly, you will recognize as "Rodolfo's Narrative" from "La Boheme.")

NANCY. *(Rapidly)* You may suddenly feel choked-off—thwarted—in the one really big thing you could have done. Then—though you love her dearly—you'll resent Ronny. You'll try not to let her see. If she loves you, she can't avoid it. Or even you yourself may not know quite what's wrong. You may simply find, all at once, that you are very empty, very unhappy. . . .

RICKY. But Nanny—look how happy Father is! *(The whistle draws closer.)*

NANCY. You can't tell much by a whistle, son.

(MAITLAND WHITE *comes in. He is forty-three, about five feet ten, and golf and squash have kept him in the pink of trim. He is not particularly handsome, but with a face and smile that—unless you be an incurable misanthrope—win you immediately. There are a few gray hairs, which* NANCY *or the barber will pull out at his next sitting. To look at him you might think him any one of a number of things. You guess that it is business, and you know that he is successful. His hands—long, slender and restless—and a kind of boyish whimsicality in him, are all that betray the artist. He wears a dinner-coat, and wears it well. He is unwrapping a large, flat package as he enters. He places it upon the center table, and carelessly drops the paper to the floor.)*

MATEY. *(To* NANCY*)* Do come here and see this Watteau print I've got for your room—— *(He sets it up against some books, and stands off to look at it, continuing his low whistling.* NANCY *goes to his side, picking up the paper en route, and slips her arm through his.)*

NANCY. Matey—you lamb—it's too enchanting!

MATEY. How pensive, how reluctant, it is. The way that man combines grace and abandon is a miraculous thing. . . .

RICKY. Father—I'm going to marry Ronny Duane——

MATEY. *(Quite unimpressed by this momentous announcement)* I call it at once a bubble, and a monument. See this lady, with her head turned, so.

You know, my dear—I think she's extraordinarily like you. . . .

NANCY. Imbecile!—Look at her nose. . . .

(MATEY *does so. Then lifts* NANCY'S *chin and studies her face for a moment.)*

MATEY. I could fix that with one line. *(Being so accessible, he kisses her.* NANCY *steals a furtive look at* RICKY, *who does not attempt to conceal his disgust.)*

RICKY. Aw—cut it out! I say, Father, that I'm going to——

MATEY. It's called "The Embarkation for Cythera"—hangs in the Louvre. *(Chuckles reminiscently.)* Remember that night the summer before we were married—when *we* embarked for Greenwich in the sailboat from Long Island?—And got becalmed halfway across? Lord! I'll never forget your mother's face, as we tiptoed in at five-thirty!

RICKY. *(Compassionately)* Poor Dad—middle age at last.

MATEY. What *is* that infant babbling about?

RICKY. It's the first time I've ever heard you brag of what a cut-up you were as a lad. Unmistakably, Dad—you're *done*. . . .

MATEY. Done, eh—? Who beat you six-love, six-three, six-two this morning?

RICKY. Oh—you're *fit* enough. It's the mind that goes first.

MATEY. *(Scornfully)* Middle age! *(None the less, he does look a little worried.)*

RICKY. I don't want to bore you—but I was breaking the news of my approaching nuptials with one Veronica Duane. . . .

MATEY. And didn't I felicitate you? How careless. Congratulations, my boy—and upon the inheritance, too.

RICKY. The—what . . . ?

MATEY. *(With a gesture)* The—uh—legacy.

RICKY. What do you mean?

MATEY. Why—er—haven't you come into a large fortune, as well?

RICKY. I haven't been advised of the fact.

MATEY. Then how do you expect to marry Ronny?

RICKY. She's got her own running-expenses, and I'm going to work.

MATEY. I sincerely trust that eventually you will.

RICKY. I want to begin right away. I'm not going abroad, Father.

(MATEY *looks to* NANCY *for an explanation. She makes a helpless gesture, as if to say, "I've done all I can." A pause.* MATEY *is dumbfounded. He turns to* RICKY, *drops his bantering air, and speaks kindly and sympathetically.)*

MATEY. Look here, old fellow, this is a little confusing. Would you mind telling me more about it?

RICKY. Why—there isn't a great deal to tell, sir. It's just that we're—very much in love, and want to be married as soon as we possibly can. I figure that if I go to work now, by Spring everything will be rosy.

MATEY. What do you plan to do?

RICKY. Same as you—the Warren Company.—Caught you, sir—you thought I'd say "sell bonds."

MATEY. And your architecture goes by the boards, eh?

RICKY. Why should it? I can study evenings, and Sundays, and finally—— *(At this patent absurdity,* MATEY *laughs.* RICKY *is injured.)* Well—

MATEY. *(Gravely)* Ricky—our method of up-
I can. . . .

bringing for you and Jean has allowed room for very few "Thou-shalt-nots." I'm not going to start ordering you about now, but there are a few things that—as an older man—I want to remind you of—— (NANCY *proceeds to examine the Watteau print more closely.)*

RICKY. Yes, Dad. . . .

MATEY. I have my own eyes, and the word of your masters at school and college, to tell me that you have a considerable gift for building design. You love the work, and you're unusually well suited to it. You need technique, and a background—and you need them badly. Three years at the Beaux-Arts will give you the best there are. . . .

RICKY. But Ronny——

MATEY. *(A little exasperated)* If Ronny won't wait for you, there'll be another girl just as charming, later on. . . . (NANNY *puts down the picture and looks at them.)*

MATEY. I want to tell you, son, that the most important thing in a man's life is his work—particularly when he has an equipment such as yours. It's hard to get going; for a while you need absolute independence—freedom to think only "I—I—I—I and my work."—After marriage that is no longer possible. From then on it's "You and I"—with the "You" first, every time. *"You* and I"——

RICKY. Sound grammar, anyway.

MATEY. *(Swiftly)* I'm not speaking idly!—And don't underestimate, either, the suffering a flouted destiny can send you. There's a course you feel cut out to take—step off it now, and you'll regret it as long as you live. (NANCY *aimlessly picks up a magazine.)*

RICKY. But—I simply can't give up Ronny—— (MATEY *stares at him, and then rises abruptly from his chair.)*

MATEY. *(Brutally)* In my opinion, any man who

sacrifices his career for the sake of a girl hasn't the backbone of—a cup-custard. (NANCY'S *head drops a little, over her magazine.* RICKY *glances at her apprehensively.)* And any girl selfish enough to permit——

RICKY. Dad—isn't this a bit rough on Mother?

MATEY. Rough on— What do you mean . . .?

NANCY. *(Very quietly)* Don't be silly, Ricky. (MATEY *looks from one to the other.)*

MATEY. But . . . ?

NANCY. I must go and dress. . . . *(To* RICKY) You'd better come too. *(She starts to cross toward the hall.)*

MATEY. Just a moment, dear—— *(Again to* RICKY) It's sheer nonsense to think you can manage two occupations—— One or the other must go. You——

RICKY. I'm afraid it's no use, Father. I've thought it all out, and my mind's made up. (MATEY *shakes his head sadly—pityingly, perhaps. Before* NANCY *reaches the door,* ETTA, *in maid's costume, enters. The kindest of all laws—that of compensations—has endowed her with lustrous hair, perfect coloring, a charming figure, and eyes to which the Blue Grot is a dirty gray. Who cares at what age the psychological tests will place her?)*

ETTA. Mr. Warren has arrived.

(Yes, here is G. T. WARREN *himself. He is about fifty-five, and partially bald—a short, plump, gusty little man, with a ready smile. He has the conceit of most self-made men, but in his case it is made amusing by his naïveté. He is, in the business vernacular, always "on his toes," and literally exudes prosperity and good nature. He speaks rapidly, and with conviction.* NANCY, MATEY *and* RICKY *rise to greet him.)*

MATEY. "—and seizing his golf-clubs, and the latest 'Cosmopolitan,' our Captain of Industry determined to relax."

WARREN. *(Briskly, as always)* Hello, White. Relax is the word. Never felt stiffer. *(Taking* NANCY'S *hand, and beaming upon her.)* And how's the little woman?

NANCY. Growing up, Mr. Warren. Delightful, having you here. I'd concluded you thought rest only for the dead. *(To* ETTA) Have Mr. Warren's chauffeur take his car to the garage. He will stay in William's quarters. *(To* WARREN) Do sit down. Would you like a pick-me-up?

WARREN. (ETTA *is in the corner of his eye)* I'll wait—— What a pretty girl! *(The pretty one goes out.)*

NANCY. Better than that, she's one of the few mortals who can get on with my old Katie. She came as a temporary, but I think I'll perpetuate her. (WARREN *advances deeper into the room, mopping his brow and adjusting his cuffs.)*

WARREN. Miserable trip, coming up. Brought that advertising man Davis far as White Plains with me. He talked saturated markets and customer resistance till I had to ask him if he handled a hot-air furnace account! *(At which he chuckles. And if you were one of his clerks, you may be certain you would roar with laughter. But——)*

NANCY. *(With a grimace to* MATEY) Mr. Warren says the quaintest things.

WARREN. Well—as I told that reporter fellow who interviewed me last week—"Smile through to success"—that's been my motto ever since I was a kid. *(To* RICKY) Hello, son—all through with college?

RICKY. The youngest living graduate. . . .

WARREN. I must mind my who's and whom's. Let's see,—it was Harvard, wasn't it?

RICKY. *(A gentle reproof)* Mr. Warren—*please*——

WARREN. My mistake! Well—I got *my* education at the University of Hard Knocks, and——

RICKY. *(An end to these wall-mottoes!)* "—and began business without a nickel in my pocket—and look at me now!" (WARREN *stares at him for a moment and then laughs.)*

WARREN. White—this is a fresh youngster of yours, but I like his spirit. Can't stand men who're afraid of me.

RICKY. You know—I like you, too. You look exactly like our old baseball trainer. If you don't mind, I think I'll come and work for you. I won't be like this in the office. At toil, I'll be very reserved. But *here—?* Well—both good fellows, wot?

WARREN. *(I can be a hale fellow, as well met as any)* Both good fellows! When can you start?

RICKY. A week from Monday. Are you on?

WARREN. Suits me. Given up your other plans?

MATEY. *(Quickly)* I don't think he's quite decided, G. T.

NANCY. He's not himself today, Mr. Warren.

RICKY. *(Scowling at them)* As a matter of fact, sir, they're full of red ants. I have *quite* decided, and I've never been more myself.

WARREN. He couldn't do better than to come with us. This is an age of business. *(He picks up the Watteau print and glances at it.)* H'm—pretty. *(Replaces it and turns again to* RICKY.) I'll put you through the production end in six months. Then the sales department. Then the—you see, we're entirely departmentalized. *(Takes pencil and paper from pocket, and sits beside* RICKY.) Look here. It's arranged like this. Here's the top: "G. T. Warren"——

RICKY. Himself!

WARREN. Then the vice-president—you know old Lawson. Then your father. Beneath us come the—

(Then—as people will—they all talk together. But unless you have an inordinate interest in business, you would better listen to NANCY *and* MATEY.)

MATEY. *(To* NANCY) I nearly forgot. Who do you think is staying with the Carharts?

(WARREN *is saying, "I'll draw it like a line of descent, showing the complete unit."* RICKY, *for want of something better, replies, "The Warren genealogy, h'm?")*

NANCY. Someone swanky.—Who?
MATEY. Geoff Nichols. He just 'phoned me.—Got back from China last week.
NANCY. *(Puzzled)* Nichols . . . ?

(WARREN *says, "Might call it that. First—Administration; then Sales; next—Distribution—with that little arrow indicating our foreign business"—at which* RICKY *appreciatively murmurs, "Europe too!")*

MATEY. You remember Geoffrey—he was one of our ushers.
NANCY. The writer person!
MATEY. Of course.—Haven't laid eyes on him for years. He's going to stop in for a moment before dinner.

(WARREN *has informed* RICKY *that "We cover the entire world" and gone on to explain: "Then Production—then finally the Purchasing De-*

partment—raw materials. There—you have it all—a three-million-dollar business. Simple, isn't it?")

NANCY. Must we talk literature to him?
MATEY. *(Laughing)* Heavens—*no!*

(RICKY, *having told his future employer that "It depends on what you call simple," brings the competitive conversation to a conclusion.)*

RICKY. You can count on young Roderick for the literary stuff. I've just gone another two inches on my Five-Foot-Shelf of Books.

WARREN. *(Giving* RICKY *the diagram)* I'll leave this with you. And if you're half the man your father is——

RICKY. *(Laconically)* Oh—I'll draw circles around Dad.

NANCY. Would you like to go to your room, Mr. Warren? The gray room, Ricky. And remember —a *stiff* shirt!

RICKY. What! Is the dear Duchess coming? *(To* WARREN) The gray room's usually reserved for ambassadors and bishops, sir, but—— *(With a deprecating gesture)* You see how you stand with us. (WARREN *laughs, and puts his hand on* RICKY'S *shoulder, preparatory to going out.)*

WARREN. *(To* MATEY) White, you've been looking completely worn out. Why not pack up and forget business for a month or two?

MATEY. The company would crack to pieces!

RICKY. Not with you and me there, would it, Chief?

WARREN. No, indeed! We've got youth on our side. It's your poor old father, who's ageing so fast. *(Slips his arm through* RICKY'S *as they cross left.)* Both good fellows, eh?

Stage Set for Act *I* of "You and I"

RICKY. *(Solemnly)* The best there are! *(They go out, and their voices die away on the favorite theme)* You know—I think I'm going to like business.

WARREN. We *need* young blood. I've always said——

MATEY. *(A little annoyed)* That amazing child!

NANCY. He's cleverer than you think. G. T. was pleased as Punch. (MATEY *seats himself in a chair.)* Oh—I've gone flat, from standing so long. *(She sinks down on the arm of* MATEY'S *chair.)* Why don't you make me go up and dress?

MATEY. *(Sternly)* Go up and dress!

NANCY. I won't!

MATEY. *(Comfortably)* You're an obstinate baggage.

NANCY. I am the wife of your bosom, and you adore me.

MATEY. Which makes you none the less obstinate, and none the less a baggage.

NANCY. Matey—you're a grand old thing—do you know it?

MATEY. I do.

NANCY. But it doesn't become you to admit it. *(A slight pause.)* I believe I'm in love with you.

MATEY. *(Impressively)* It is my fatal fascination. *(Suddenly troubled)* Nanny—have I been looking done in lately—or done up—or done anyway?

NANCY. Why—*no! (She turns his head around and scrutinizes his face.)* A little tired, perhaps. *(She finds a gray hair, and with squinting eye and set mouth, proceeds to separate it from the others.)* Here's another gray one. Out you come, false prophet! (MATEY *submits to the operation. The offending member is held up for his inspection.) Voila!*—As the driven snow. . . . (MATEY *laughs, a little nervously.)*

MATEY. Any other signs?
NANCY. Of what?
MATEY. Senility.
NANCY. None but the fact that you are being unusually childish.
MATEY. Well—G. T. and the infant both spoke of it.
NANCY. Of what?
MATEY. My premature decline.
NANCY. *(Lovingly)* Matey—you idiot!
MATEY. Well, after all—here I am, forty odd—life's half over. . . .
NANCY. I never heard such nonsense! You're in the very prime of life. . . .
MATEY. *(With a grimace)* "Prime"—wretched word. Soon I'll be "spry." What a week it's been! Went to the mat with G. T. again yesterday. He can't seem to get it into his head that if we're to keep up our expansion, we've got to advertise in a big way—like Colgate's. . . .
NANCY. Of course we have——
MATEY. I've been at him for years. Our appropriation is fifty thousand, where it ought to be five hundred. And he says he won't increase it a nickel until he finds a way to advertise the entire line as a unit. Which is simple rot.
NANCY. He's a tight-fisted old fool.
MATEY. No, he's not. He's merely obtuse.
NANCY. You put things so beautifully, my dear.
MATEY. Honestly, Nanny—I get so fed-up at times, I could throw over the whole works.
NANCY. *(With genuine sympathy)* Poor lamb. Seriously—what about a holiday? It's years since we've been abroad.
MATEY. The market's shot to pieces. We can't afford it—not if we're to send Ricky.
NANCY. But—you know—he's not going.

MATEY. You think he's actually in earnest about the factory?

NANCY. I'm almost certain he is. But perhaps—on the side—he can——

MATEY. "On the side!" Heaven save him from it! His one hope for peace is to forget it entirely—*(Shaking his head sadly.)* Oh—it's criminal for that boy to give up his career. *(A slight pause.)*

NANCY. Was it—criminal—for *you* to, Matey? *(Another pause. Then* MATEY *laughs easily.)*

MATEY. So *that's* what he meant! *(Reassuringly)* It's quite different with us—quite.

NANCY. *Is* it?

MATEY. *(With spirit)* Of course!

NANCY. *(Dubiously)* Well—I'm glad to know *that. (From the hall is heard a man's voice saying, "Well—if people* will *leave their doors open they can expect other people to walk in without ringing—so here I am!")* I wonder if that's——

(Quite right—it is GEOFFREY NICHOLS. *He is* MATEY'S *age, taller, very slight and with a most engaging manner. In comparison with the other successful literary men of your acquaintance, his affectations are very few.)*

MATEY. Geoff! By Gad—this is fine!

NICHOLS. *(Taking his hand delightedly)* Matey—you pig! If you don't look prosperous! And this is—Mrs. Matey—— *(Crooking a speculative finger at* NANCY.) Your name is—don't tell me, now—your name is—Nancy! And you were the prettiest bride ever I saw. What a wedding! I was frightfully sorry about that punch-bowl—I should have known that I couldn't balance it on my nose. By Jove, you seem *two* years older, instead of—— *(He covers his eyes with his hands, in mock dismay.)* Oh—I mustn't say it—I can feel my shroud as I do. . . .

NANCY. You delightful man.

NICHOLS. *(To* MATEY*)* I begged you not to marry. I eat my words. I behold the ideal wife.

NANCY. Can nothing induce you to stay and dine?

NICHOLS. It would be writing my doom with the Carharts.

NANCY. Then do come to us for next week-end.

NICHOLS. I'm so sorry. I sail Wednesday on the *Majestic.*

NANCY. Pity us.

NICHOLS. But Monday—join me in town for dinner and the theater—I've seats for the *Chauve Souris.*

NANCY. *(To* MATEY*)* Are you free?

MATEY. As these United States.

NANCY. *(To* NICHOLS*)* We should be charmed. Now I simply must re-drape myself for dinner. You want to talk, anyway. Don't go till I come down, will you? *(*NICHOLS *bows, and with her most gracious smile* NANCY *goes out.* MATEY *offers* NICHOLS *a cigarette, which he accepts.)*

NICHOLS. Well—"home is the sailor, home from the sea"—and all that jolly rot.

MATEY. Geoff—it's been twenty years at least.

NICHOLS. I demand a recount!

MATEY. I last broke bread with you in the Spring of 'Ninety-nine. . . .

NICHOLS. My Victorian Memoirs. *(They seat themselves.)*

MATEY. Where *have* you been?

NICHOLS. Everywhere! I'm a veritable flea for travel. London is my old lady—Paris, my mistress—and Rome—ah, Rome—my saint in décolleté! *(*MATEY *laughs, a little enviously, and begins sketching, absently, on the back of a magazine)*—and what have the long years held for you, as they say?

MATEY. Oh—here and New York—business as usual.

NICHOLS. What different lives we've had.

MATEY. Haven't we?

NICHOLS. *(Reflectively)* And yet at twenty we were much the same. Twenty—the incendiary age, Matey. I was going to set the world on fire with my novels—your match was a paint-brush.

MATEY. And I gave up my painting to marry Nancy Lyon. . . .

NICHOLS. While I forsook sweet Kitty Nash to wed with an ink-pot! A pair of jilts, we two! Well—what do you think of *your* bargain?

MATEY. I've come out the winner, Geoff.

NICHOLS. And so have I!

MATEY. Impossible!—I've a happy home—sufficient leisure—a regular income—two fine, spoiled children—and a wife that's a simple miracle. Trump them, if you can!

NICHOLS. *(Gayly, with the gesture of laying cards on the table, one by one)* The world's my home—every hour of my time is my own—I'll match my income with yours any day!—And as for your last three items, I say what Bacon said: "A man with wife and children has given hostages to Fortune!"

MATEY. But old lady Fortune has done me rather well.

NICHOLS. Oh—she has her favorite slaves. But freedom's the thing! As Shaw said to me one day last April—dash it—what *was* it he said?—At any rate, it was simply convulsing.

MATEY. But how on earth have you done any work?

NICHOLS. Work? Why, every new experience is material. Wherever I go, my typewriter follows. No worries, no responsibilities—just *life*,—the one life I have—spiced and succulent.

MATEY. While I—day after day—"Nine to five—nine to five."

NICHOLS. Those words are the business man's epitaph.

MATEY. *(Determined to be sprightly)* Oh—one has one's moments. Even a business man. (NICHOLS *glances at* MATEY'S *sketch.)*

NICHOLS. But as I remember, you showed amazing promise. I've known artists with wives—with children, even. Why didn't you go on with it? (MATEY *returns the magazine to the table, and pockets the pencil.)*

MATEY. Well, you see, Nancy and I married ridiculously young—neither of us rich, but both accustomed to a certain standard of living.—A regular income became pretty much of a necessity.

NICHOLS. And you put it off. Tsch—what a shame——

MATEY. *(Reluctantly)* Perhaps—I don't know. Sometimes—when I think that I haven't yet done the thing I wanted to do—my forty-three years do seem rather futile and misspent. It's been particularly salty today. My boy Roderick, for whom I've expected great things—— *(He shifts uneasily in his chair.)* Oh, well—it's the old story over again.

NICHOLS. But some phases of your life must be very interesting. Now business is not without its—

MATEY. Geoff, business is a dump for dreams. I believe every fourth man in it has something shut down in him. You can see it in their faces. Some of them wanted to paint, like me,—some to write, to sing—to be doctors, lawyers—God bless me, even preachers! But expediency ordered it otherwise. And now most of them will die in the traces, poor devils . . . die of market reports—Babsonitis—hardening of the soul——

NICHOLS. Ah, yes— as some one says, "Most men lead lives of quiet desperation."

Matey. *(Softly)* "Quiet desperation." *(He rises, sharply)* By God—here's one who's fed-up with it! I've a good mind to chuck business *now*—and go to painting! (Nichols *looks somewhat alarmed; this is being taken too literally.)*

Nichols. You're not serious . . . ?

Matey. So serious that the turn of a hair would decide it.

Nichols. *(Rising after a helpless pause)* You must realize that the—uh—artistic life—has its *dis*-advantages, too. One's laurels are so insecure. Popularity is such a fickle thing . . .

Matey. Who said anything about popularity?

Nichols. *(Shrugging)* One might as well live, as not.

Matey. If you do good work, you make quite enough.

Nichols. But my income isn't half what it's reputed to be! And the irregular hours! Lord, Matey—my nerves are chaos.

Matey. Mine are paralyzed.

Nichols. And look at me!—My age—and still flitting about from pillar to post like a gouty bumblebee . . .

Matey. In motion, at any rate. I never leave the ground. (Nichols, *with a profound sigh, sinks into a comfortable chair.)*

Nichols. *(The fraud)* What I wouldn't give for a home like this—and children—and a wife like your Nancy!

Matey. You have your Art . . .

Nichols. She's not so sweet as Kitty Nash!—And if it weren't for her and her importunities, I might have Kitty now—and a home that *is* a home.

Matey. You've compensations . . .

Nichols. No, Matey. I suppose I should have, if I could honestly feel that art—true art—was the gainer for my sacrifice. But a popular novelist!

Oh—don't you suppose *I* know what my stuff is worth? *(He continues with deep feeling)* I give you my word—there's no such hell on earth as that of the man who knows himself doomed to mediocrity in the work he loves—whatever it may be. You love painting—you think you could paint great pictures.—Well—go on thinking—but don't try it. No! No!—You've done well in business—be wise, and stick to it.

MATEY. I am stuck.

NICHOLS. What are you, anyway?

MATEY. Why—uh—I'm a manufacturer . . .

NICHOLS. What do you make?

MATEY. *(This is painful)* Oh—uh—various things . . .

NICHOLS. But what's the—*pièce de résistance,* so to speak?

MATEY. *(Very painful indeed)* Well—uh—I suppose one would say—uh—*soap* . . .

NICHOLS. Soap! God!—You can get your *teeth* into soap!

MATEY. *(Cynically)* You can into *ours.* It proclaims itself made of only the purest edible fats.

NICHOLS. Believe me, I envy you——

MATEY. But you've no idea of the—*hunger* I have, to be painting.

NICHOLS. Can't you find time to daub a bit on the side?

MATEY. Business life has no side. It's one dimension. Try it and see. Ah—if only I could get free of it—altogether free of it, for a while. To feel a brush in my hand again—to see a picture grow under my eyes—to create—good God!—something other than a cake of soap.

NICHOLS. By Jove—if it's *good* soap . . .

MATEY. *(Interrupting)* But this house—and the apartment in town—and the servants—and the children to educate! Of course it's impossible,—plainly impossible.

NICHOLS. And lucky for you that it is. Forget it, Matey, forget it——

MATEY. I wish to heaven I could!

(NANCY'S *entrance—a vision in evening dress—brings the men to their feet.)*

NICHOLS. Ah—*vous êtes adorable!*

NANCY. *Mille fois merci, cher Monsieur.*

NICHOLS. *(Glancing at his watch)* I'd no idea it was so late. *(Going to the door, followed by* MATEY.) I shall look forward to Monday night. Sherry's at seven-thirty?

NANCY. Me, and my man Matey; prompt, as always.

NICHOLS. *(At door) Dieu soit béni d'avoir conçu une aussi ravissante personne*——

NANCY. *(Which serves him right)* The new slippers of my old grandmother are red. (NICHOLS *laughs, and he and* MATEY *go out.* NANCY *moves toward the desk, humming—and stops halfway with a perplexed frown. Continues to desk, again humming. Seats herself and begins to finish letter.* MATEY *reënters, and, going to the table, stands there with his fingers resting upon it, staring down at the Watteau print, rapt in thought.* NANCY *speaks without turning.)* Enjoy your talk?

MATEY. *(Absently)* What—?—Oh—uh—*yes*—very much . . . *(His voice trails off)* . . . very much . . . *(A pause.)* What a fascinating time Nichols has had of it!

NANCY. *(A few more lines, and* JEAN'S *letter will be finished)* M-m-m—I must read something of his . . .

MATEY. *(Half to himself)* "Hostages to Fortune." *(A pause; lower)* "Most men lead lives of quiet desperation."

NANCY. What, dear . . . (MATEY *looks a little startled.)*

MATEY. I said, "Most men lead lives of quiet desperation." (NANCY, *puzzled, glances over her shoulder at him. Turns again, reflectively biting the end of her pen. Then cheerfully continues her writing.)*

NANCY. Well—so long as they're quiet about it—let's—let them go right ahead—shall we . . . ? (MATEY, *deep in thought, does not answer.* NANCY *seals the note, addresses it, stamps it with a bang, and goes to him. She puts her hands upon his shoulders, and faces him about.)* Matey—you sweet old thing—what *is* the matter?

MATEY. *(With an attempt at a smile)* Oh—nothing. . . . *(He cups her elbows in the palms of his hands for an instant and then leaves her.)*

NANCY. *(After a thoughtful pause)* Dear—it seems to me that you've about everything that a person could desire. We've—most of the good things of life—health—position—enough money—a happy family. *(She hesitates)* And we've—each other. Nor is ours the tame, settled love most people have at forty. Some blessed good fortune has kept the keen edge on it. I love my children—but compared to you—oh, Matey! *(A little laugh.)* I fancy—there's more woman in me, than mother. . . . *(A pause;* MATEY *says nothing.* NANCY *is chilled.)* You have been unusually successful in your work. What more could any man ask—than *you have* . . . ?

MATEY. *(Impatiently, but with intense suffering)* Nanny—*Nanny*—what *do you* know about it! (NANCY *catches her breath sharply, holds it a moment, and then lets it go.)*

NANCY. *(Almost in a whisper)* I suppose—you know—it—just about knocks the heart out of me, to hear you say that. . . . *(She waits for a response. None comes. She clenches her fist, half raises her arms, and throws back her head, in pain.)* Oh—this *can't* be you and I! *(Her arms drop again lifelessly. A moment's silence. She regains her composure, and going to* MATEY, *speaks to him in a matter-of-fact voice.)* Maitland—as you love me—there's something I want you to do.

MATEY. What is it?

NANCY. *(Directly)* Leave business for a year. Get leave of absence, if possible. Otherwise, resign . . .

MATEY. *(Affecting to be puzzled)* But—my dear—*why* . . . ?

NANCY. *(With an impatient gesture)* Oh—*please!* Do you think I've had all these years of you—to be fooled by pretense now? I've known for a *long* time that you weren't happy—and why you weren't. But I've *not* known—quite how much it meant to you. I want you to devote the year to painting.

MATEY. *(Indulgently)* It's a nice idea, Nanny, but—— *(His gesture includes the house, the cars, the servants.)*

NANCY. *(Rapidly)* We'll give up the apartment. We'll stay out here over the winter. One car—and run it ourselves. We'll keep Katie and Etta—and let the others go. I'll do the upstairs myself. Ricky will be in business—no longer an expense. My own income will be enough to dress Jean and pay her school bills.

MATEY. You understand—I've very little outside of my salary?

NANCY. Little—but plenty for us. We'll economize in everything—— *(She looks at the three lighted lamps with a smile.)* We'll—begin with the electric lights. The front attic can be made into a studio. . . .

MATEY. People would think I'd lost my mind.

NANCY. *(Scornfully)* People!

MATEY. I suppose they wouldn't have to know. But G. T.——

NANCY. *(Quickly)* Tell him it's—personal research work.

MATEY. And if the research finds nothing?

NANCY. Matey—if you don't still think the bird in the bush worth any two in the hand, you might as well die.

MATEY. *(Smiling)* That's very deft, indeed. But I'm *not* going to be bullied into——

NANCY. Nobody's bullying you.

MATEY. Well—we'll think it over. Perhaps—by-and-by . . .

NANCY. We'll do nothing of the sort. You must tell G. T. tonight. How long would it take you to wind up your affairs?

MATEY. Why, I always keep them arranged, so that if anything should happen to me——

NANCY. Splendid! Something *has* happened to you: You've decided to start painting the first of the month.

MATEY. *(After a thoughtful pause)* Nope. It's no use—the whole thing's too absurd.

NANCY. This isn't a whim. If you won't do it for your own happiness, perhaps you will for mine. (MATEY *glances at her quickly.)*

MATEY. *(In spite of himself)* By Gad, Nanny—you *are* a brick!

NANCY. *(Enigmatically)* Maybe I'm not a brick at all. Maybe I'm—just fighting for something I thought I had.

MATEY. *(Scoffing)* *Thought* you had!

NANCY. At any rate, you've got to do it. . . . *(This should settle it.)*

MATEY. *(But it doesn't)* No, Nanny, *no.*—Think of the practical side—the expense.

NANCY. I did. My plans for economy quite astonished me!

MATEY. They might apply out here. Not in town.

NANCY. Town . . . ?

MATEY. *(Lamely)* I'd—uh—I'd naturally do portraits, wouldn't I?—And that necessitates models, doesn't it?

NANCY. Well?

MATEY. Well—the countryside's not precisely dotted with them. (NANCY *amusedly shakes her head over him.)*—And that's only one objection.

NANCY. I've seldom heard a lamer one. If I can get servants to come to the country, why can't you get models?

MATEY. You don't realize that—— (NANCY *presses a button in the wall.)*

NANCY. Matey, I realize that the thing of main importance is for you to begin your painting at once.

MATEY. I never saw such a devil for speed.

NANCY. Give yourself time to think up objections, and you won't start at all. If I can manage with a temporary maid, you can with a temporary model.

MATEY. Some pinched, painted relic, I suppose—

NANCY. Not at all. (ETTA *enters, the apotheosis of young, fresh beauty.)*

MATEY. It's impossible, Nanny. It's——

ETTA. You rang?

NANCY. Yes.—Etta—I—uh—I presume you never posed as a model? (ETTA'S *mouth opens in astonishment. She looks from one to the other.)*

ETTA. Why, *Ma'am!* Of *course* I didn't! Who said that I——?

NANCY. There, Etta—no one. I merely——

ETTA. *(Is a pretty girl never safe from scandal?)* Didn't I not bring the best of references? Wasn't

I not three years in my last place?—And two in the —a *model!* Why, I—— (MATEY *is studying her, crimson lake in his eye.)*

NANCY. You know—a model may be a model, and still be—er—*model*. . . .

ETTA. *(Desperately)* But Mrs. White—really—I tell you that——

NANCY. Yes—I comprehend. You have never been a model—never, in the *slightest* degree. Now, what I am attempting to tell you, is that Mr. White expects to spend the next year painting—in the attic . . . (ETTA *regards* MATEY *as if he had gone insane. He is most uncomfortable under her scrutiny)* . . . which will be made over into a studio. *(To* MATEY) Do you think Etta would serve your purpose?

MATEY. *(Off his guard)* Why, you know—it's quite extraordinary—— *(Then, with attempted nonchalance)* Oh—I dare say she might do to start with.

NANCY. *(To* ETTA) If you will consent to remain here in the country with us this winter, and pose for a few hours each day——

ETTA. *(Gently)* I am sorry, Ma'am——

NANCY. Just a moment!—I shall increase your wages, and help you with your work.

ETTA. *(Firmly)* No, Ma'am—I could not consider it. Not for all the money in the world.

NANCY. *(Frankly puzzled)* But—I don't understand. Would you mind telling us why? (ETTA *hesitates, peering at* MATEY.) You may be quite frank.

ETTA. Well—I do not like to say nothing, but the man of the house in the third last place I was in made advances that was—advances that *were*—most unwelcome. You know how careful a girl has got to be—specially when Nature has blessed her with looks like mine. I can usually tell by their eyes——

(She tries to get a look at MATEY'S, *but the clever man outwits her.)* I am not saying nothing against Mr. White. So far, he has behaved like a real gennulmun. But if I should ferget myself to the extent of—oh, you know what artists are—they, and sailors——

MATEY. I think I can practically assure you that my admirable conduct will continue indefinitely.

ETTA. *(Cannily)* You cannot tell what'll happen, if you take to paintin'. I know all about artists: women to them are as tinders to the flames. . . .

NANCY. There's the Hearst of it, Matey! *(To* ETTA) I shall vouch for Mr. White. He is not at all—combustible. Come now, will you—or will you not?

ETTA. No, Ma'am—I cannot do it. I would like to help you, but I simply dassent—do not dare to—do it.

NANCY. Very well. You are an extremely silly girl. That's all—— (ETTA *turns to go out.)* Oh—by the way—in the morning please pack that old foulard of mine, and the gray crêpe de chine. I wish them sent to the C. O. S.

ETTA. *(Heartbroken at having to wear something less becoming next Thursday)* But—didn't you say——?

NANCY. I was mistaken. I thought you were more obliging.

ETTA. But I *am* obliging——

NANCY. You have given me no indication of it. (ETTA *looks searchingly at* MATEY. *He shifts uneasily in his chair.)*

ETTA. But Ma'am—I want to *improve* myself. I want to be a lady, Mrs. White. In all my spare time I read books. I study you and your friends, and seek to em-ulate you. . . .

NANCY. *(Kindly, after a disconcerted pause)* Thank you, Etta. But surely every lady should know something about art. Now Mr. White is a very charming, cultivated man—— (MATEY *rises abruptly.)* Your hours with him would be a great opportunity for you.

ETTA. *(With difficulty)* Well—well, there is one thing we would have to have an understanding on: none of his gennulmun friends could come in while I—while I was—was—— *(She is unable to go on.)*

NANCY. *(Puzzled)* While you were——? *(It suddenly dawns upon her, but she controls her mirth.)* But I cannot see your objection. I should think you would look very charming in your—— *(To* MATEY) Do you think one of my *dresses* will do—or shall we have one made? (ETTA *looks first surprised, then considerably relieved as she echoes the wonderful word "dresses.")*

MATEY. Better have it made—— (ETTA'S *face lights up.)*

NANCY. *(Smiling)* Well, Etta——?

ETTA. *(Beaming)* Oh, *yes,* Ma'am—I didn't understand. Yes, Ma'am—with pleasure.—And any of his friends that want to look on——

NANCY. Well—that's better.—You may bring the tray in now—five glasses. Mr. White will give you more explicit directions later. (ETTA *fixes* MATEY *with an appraising stare, borne with difficulty by him. She finally goes out.* NANCY *now laughs without constraint.)* Oh—Matey—I couldn't have stood it a minute longer! Virtue in jeopardy! What a brave fight she put up!

MATEY. *(Shaking himself)* Whew!—I feel like the Seven Deadlies! I could do with a cocktail. . . .

NANCY. They're coming.—You know, I don't think she's at all certain about you yet.

MATEY. I hope she understands that I'm going to paint, and not conduct a finishing-school. Seriously, though, Nanny—we're insane to rush into this thing as if——

NANCY. *(Her merriment gone at once) Rush?*— After twenty *years?* My *dear!* (WARREN'S *voice is heard from the hall.)*

WARREN. *(Expounding it)* So you see, the entire organization is composed of interlocking units—

MATEY. *(Opening his hand to release them)* All right! There they go—the two-in-the-hand! We're off for the bird-in-the-bush! (NANCY *exclaims in joy.)*

RICKY. *(Seriously)* I think that cost-accounting system is a knockout, Sir. *(He and* WARREN *come in, dressed for dinner.)*

NANCY. Mr. Warren, Maitland has something important to tell you—— (ETTA *enters, with a tray of glasses and a cocktail-shaker.)*

WARREN. *(To* MATEY) What about? No business, I hope. (ETTA *places the tray on the table.* MATEY *begins to shake the shaker.* ETTA *watches him like a hawk. He tries to cover his embarrassment.)*

MATEY. *(Giving shaker a final shake)* I'll tell you later. Prepare for the worst! *(To* ETTA) I'll serve them. . . . *(Still she watches him, transfixed. He loses patience.)* I say *I* will *serve* them! (ETTA *goes out.* MATEY *fills glasses, and gives one to* NANCY *and one to* WARREN. RONNY *appears in hall. She is in evening dress and leaves her wrap in* ETTA'S *hands as she sails past her.)*

NANCY. We must hurry through these. The birds will be ruined. *(Nobody notices* RONNY.)

RONNY. *(In self-defense)* Good evening, Ronny—— (RICKY *rapidly reaches her side.)*

NANCY. My dear—how sweet you look!

RONNY. *(Why not be honest?)* I think I look pretty well, myself. . . .

RICKY. Plain face, but a nifty dresser.

RONNY. Hello, Handsome—I hardly knew you. Aren't you clean!

RICKY. Dad's in the business.

NANCY. This is our friend Miss Duane, Mr. Warren.

WARREN. Very glad to meet you, Miss Duane.

RONNY. *(In her cool manner with strangers)* How do you do? (RICKY *quickly whispers something to her. She goes to* WARREN, *smiling graciously. Extending a slim hand to him, she speaks as if she had not heard the name)* Oh—Mr. *Warren!* How delightful! I hear you're to have a new laborer next week . . . ?

WARREN. Indeed I am—*Rocky!* (RICKY *scowls at the name.)* He begins in what we call "The Kitchen."

RONNY. How amusing! I should think he'd be simply priceless, mixing cold cream. He's such an oil-can as it is, that——

RICKY. Dad! Give her a cocktail—quick! *(He takes one from* MATEY *and gives it to her.)*

RONNY. *(Accepting it)* Good dog. . . . (MATEY *gives* RICKY *another, and takes one for himself.)*

NANCY. *(To* WARREN) Will he need an apron?

WARREN. White overalls!

RONNY. *(Slowly sipping her cocktail)* Little Purity—with a lily in his hair. . . .

RICKY. *(Disregarding her and raising his glass)* Here's to bigger and better soap!

WARREN. *(To* RONNY) Never you mind—Rocky and I—— (RONNY *all but chokes at the repetition of the name.)*

RICKY. *(Politely)* The name is "Ricky," Sir.

WARREN. Ricky and I are going to smile through to success—aren't we, old fellow?

RICKY. Chief—we're going to laugh out loud!

MATEY. *(From table)* Here, G. T.—give me your glass. (WARREN *shakes his head, and he and* NANCY *place their empty glasses upon the tray.)*

RICKY. *(To* RONNY) That's Mr. Warren's motto: "Use our Pearly Paste, and Smile with Confidence."

RONNY. *(Over her cocktail)* Gosh, you're coarse.

RICKY. *(Aggrieved)* I *must* say, I fail to see anything coarse about——

NANCY. Never mind, Ricky. *(To* WARREN *and* MATEY) Are we ready . . . ? (NANCY, WARREN *and* MATEY *go to the door.* RONNY *is finishing her cocktail.)*

RICKY. C'mon, Beau'ful—lap it up!

RONNY. *(Putting down her glass)* M-m-m-m—I shall be charming at dinner.

(MATEY *stands at the door to let them all pass, and turns to follow.* NANCY *reënters hurriedly, and in reply to his questioning glance says, "I'll come in a minute." He goes out and* NANCY *tours the room, turning out the lamps one by one.* RICKY *calls from the dining-rom)*

RICKY. *(Imperatively)* Dear-r-r-r-est——!

NANCY. *(Singing it out, with a falling inflection)* Com-m-m-m-m-ing——! *(She turns out the last lamp, and is rapidly crossing the darkened room to the lighted hall, as—)*

THE CURTAIN FALLS

ACT II

You may be a little out of breath when you come into MATEY'S *Studio, for it is in the attic, and you must climb a flight of steep steps to get there. The stairway is in a small recess at the back, and we shall see your head first. The small door at the left—as you enter—is the entrance to the playroom.*

The Studio is a spacious, rectangular room with a large dormer window cut in the back wall, and in the right wall two smaller windows through which may be seen the tip of an apple branch, in bloom. The curtains at the windows show NANCY'S *touch—this room has been great fun for her, and she has been very successful in keeping out of it any suggestion of the "arty."*

At one side, there is a long refectory table, covered with a "runner" and bearing two wrought-iron sconces, each containing six white candles. By the large window there are bookshelves and a comfortable sofa. Chairs ad lib.—but space is the thing.

Being essentially a workroom, there is a dais with a throne-chair for the model, an easel (turned away from the front), a small work-table with brushes, paints, etc., and a life-sized lay-figure (a great family joke, by the way) which sprawls upon the floor in a thoroughly gauche manner.

With the exception of a bearskin and a small rug, the floor is uncovered. On the walls you will see Hokusai's "Fujiyama" and "The Wave" and very good prints they are. There are also two mounted heads of wild goats, upon the smaller of which a red Spanish berèt is set at a rakish angle.

The fact that the studio was once an attic is still apparent, to the close observer, through the medium of only partially hidden trunks, and a dappled-gray hobby-horse.

It is late the following May—about four in the afternoon. MATEY, *in a smock, with a small daub of paint on his cheek, is busily painting at his easel.* ETTA *poses in the throne-chair. She wears a simple, exquisite afternoon-dress, and a small string of pearls at her throat. Her hands rest in her lap. Her hair is dressed most becomingly, and the transformation into a charming lady of unusual grace and beauty is quite complete. For a few moments* MATEY *paints silently. Gradually* ETTA'S *features lose their repose. An expression of acute suffering grows in her eyes. She wrinkles her nose and sets her teeth. Finally—*

ETTA. *(At the end of her tether, poor dear)* Mr. White—I have jest *got* to do it . . .

MATEY. *(Patiently ceasing his work)* All right, Etta—go ahead—— (ETTA, *with a great sigh of relief, vigorously scratches her nose.)* Would you like to rest for a moment?

ETTA. Oh—may I . . . ? (MATEY *gestures acquiescence, lays brushes on work-table, and goes to the open windows, where the bees are humming among the apple blossoms.) Sech* a relief! (MATEY *picks a small sprig of blossoms and presents it to her.)*

MATEY. Here—this will refresh you. *(For his own refreshment, he lights a cigarette.* ETTA *inhales the fragrance of the blossoms and regards the twig lovingly.)*

ETTA. Oh—thank you. Mm-m-m-m—I jest simply love apple-blossoms.

MATEY. You have an unhappy knack of pronouncing "just" and "such" as if they were spelled with "e's" instead of "u's."

ETTA. "Just"—"such."

MATEY. That's better. . . .

ETTA. *(Diffidently)* It's nice, being a lady, Mr. White. *(Lest he misunderstand her)* Of course, I *am* a lady. But—*(Looking down at her dress and fingering her pearls)*—I mean a de luxe one—like those that come to see Mrs. White. How I'd love to be like they are—and talk the way they do!

MATEY. *(Absently, as he studies the portrait)* You should practise—in private. It's only the mouth that bothers me now.—" 'The Portrait of a Lady,' by an Unknown Artist"—— *(Reflectively)* When we've sold it to some great lover of art, *then* perhaps I'll sign it—— *(Softly)* *When*—— *(He extinguishes his cigarette and picks up his brush and pallette.)* Come on—are you ready?

ETTA. Jest—*just* a minute. . . . *(Once more she strikes her pose, and* MATEY *silently continues his painting.)* Is it really almost done?

MATEY. *(Engrossed)* It may be two minutes—it may be two days.

ETTA. I could jest cry, I could——

MATEY. Please don't—I'm no good at marines. *(He paints rapidly for a few moments. Then stands off and regards her quizzically from several positions.)* Softer lines around the mouth—— *(Just to make it sure, she grins.)* No! No!—You know better than that! *Soft,* I said. *(He studies her attempt.)* Bring your eyes into it. . . . *(He shakes his head hopelessly, but continues to paint. Suddenly a little laugh escapes her.)* What are you laughing at?

ETTA. It just struck me funny—here you've been trying for months to make that look like me, when with a camera you could get it perfect in a jiffy. (MATEY *stares at her, speechless.)*

MATEY. *(Softly)* Oh, my God. . . . *(With increased vehemence)* You sit there prattling of cameras, when you ought to be thanking heaven for the dignity that's done you! Don't you see the chance you've got? Who was Helen of Troy but a pretty thing with convenient morals? Who was—La Gioconda but a woman with a smile? If there'd been no Homer to sing of Helen, no Leonardo to fix that smile forever with his brush, they'd both be dead and forgotten as—*(He picks up the twig of apple-blossoms)*—as this will be tomorrow! And—*(She is staring at him without a trace of comprehension in her face)*—and you haven't the faintest idea what I'm talking about. *(He throws the twig out of the window, falls into thought for a moment, and then speaks again, with restrained but poignant feeling)* Is there nothing that will make you understand what this means? *(He indicates the portrait)* Can't you realize that what is here is more than merely you and my work? That in it there's a—spirit that can strike life into—*(He holds the prostrate lay-figure up to view)*—a lump of sawdust, like this You?—Why, it can immortalize you! Let me see in your face—joy—wonder—consecration! *(A big order:* ETTA *bites her lip anxiously.)*

ETTA. All at once, or—one at a time?

(MATEY *shakes his head, as if to say, "No use," and placing the lay-figure at the foot of the easel, again ponders a means whereby he may instil into his subject's spirit a something that will show in her face. Finally an idea strikes him, and bringing a high stool to a position directly in front of* Etta, *he sits upon it, and proceeds to draw for her as alluring a verbal picture as he can.)*

Matey. Now listen! You want to be a lady, don't you? Well—I'll make you one. Think—up on Fifth Avenue there's a palatial white edifice. There, in a long, high room lavishly embellished with palms and other potted plants, *you* sit, *you,* Etta—the hostess at a most de luxe reception. The room is filled with fashionable ladies in their jewels and furs and orchids. Their stylish escorts stand about with silk hats in their white-gloved hands. From everywhere, they've come thronging to pay you homage—earls and dukes and duchesses—ambassadors and their wives . . . *(Can it be that he, too, has read "The Earl's Revenge"?)* And for all time, you will live in their memories. In the far capitals of the world exquisite women will sit before their glasses in costly boudoirs, and whisper sadly, "Ah—if I were as lovely as she!" Handsome men, on whose word the fates of empires hang, will pause in the middle of an important stroke of diplomacy, and sigh to themselves, "Ah—what would I not do, for the love of such a lady!" You will be with them at their rich dinners—their gorgeous balls. Books will be written about you, and elegantly bound in leather. And you will hold your queenly sway, not for a season or two, like other fine ladies—but for a hundred years, *two* hundred! You, Etta, *you*—the finest lady of them all! *(His voice sinks)* Can you—see it?—*feel* it——? *(A look of wonderment has grown in her eyes. She sits entranced, her face transfigured with a kind of gracious, queenly joy.* Matey *draws a deep and grateful breath and rising, goes slowly to the easel, with his eyes still upon her, repeating softly)* The—finest—lady—of—them—all—— *(He paints rapid-*

ly, but with infinite care, looking from her to the portrait and back again. A few more strokes—and tossing his brush in the air, he exclaims jubilantly) There! By the Lord Harry, we've got it! Etta—you *Love*—we've *got* it! (ETTA *comes out of her trance and starts forward.* MATEY *seizes her hand and drags her to the portrait.)* Look—it's done! *(She gazes at the marvel with widening eyes, while* MATEY *gleefully daubs a sign, "Fresh Paint," on a piece of cardboard.)*

ETTA. Oh, if that isn't simply the grandest thing! And to think that it's me—a lady like that! Oh, *isn't* she lovely! (MATEY *places the sign on the corner of the easel, thereby eliciting a giggle from* ETTA *—not a difficult achievement.)* Just as if it was a park bench! Mr. White—you do the *cutest* things. *(In sheer jubilance,* MATEY *takes her hands and dances her around.)*

MATEY. *(To the tune of "Round and Round the Mulberry Bush")* It's done! It's done! It's done —done—done—so early in the morning!

ETTA. *(Breathlessly)* But it's *afternoon!*

MATEY. So early in the *morning!* (ETTA, *at first a reluctant partner, at length abandons herself to the celebration.)*

MATEY *and* ETTA. *(As they dance around)* It's done! It's done, done, done—so early in the morning!

(NANCY *enters, attired—heaven save us!—in a short black housedress and a white apron.)*

NANCY. The ceilings may hold out downstairs. But the odds are against it. What is it all about?

MATEY. *(Ten years off his age)* History, my dear! I've finished the portrait! We were celebrating the dawn of a new epoch in American Art—

(He performs a pirouette)—So early in the morning!

NANCY. Finished . . . ? Oh—wonderful—! *(She goes swiftly to the portrait and regards it with shining eyes.)* Matey—I could go on my knees to it. . . .

MATEY. *(Huskily)* I'm—glad it pleases you, dear——

NANCY. *Pleases* me!—Can't you see what's in my silly eyes? *(She blinks back the tears, and laughs joyfully.)* There—I'm a fool. Oh!—Those pearls might be alive! You know, one feels awfully cocky, with a husband who can—— *(She sees* ETTA *staring at her and trying to control her laughter.)* What is it you find so diverting?

ETTA. *(With the air of the lady* MATEY *has painted)* Your appearance. It amuses one.—Chawming, though—really *quate* chawming. . . .

NANCY. You'd better go finish cleaning the silver. (ETTA, *somewhat diminished, goes out.)* Matey—you've simply ruined her. She'll serve the children's dinner guests tonight like a queen throwing pence to the poor.

MATEY. *(Amused)* Why not have a buffet supper up here, instead? (NANCY *is struck by the idea.)*

NANCY. May we? Splendid! They'd love it. And incidentally, with all this—atmosphere, we can figure on less food.

MATEY. How many are they?

NANCY. Sixteen, counting you and me—the prospective ushers and bridesmaids, you know. They've hit on rather a sweet way of announcing it at Ronny's dance. Ricky's to be a troubadour, and Ronny a Seventeenth Century lady. I've a costume for you. . . .

MATEY. *(As he scrapes paint from the palette)* Good.—How *are* the funds, dear?

NANCY. They haven't been lower since the day after our wedding-trip.

MATEY. Thank God there's a picture for sale—and a dividend due.

NANCY. *(Regarding the pile of mail on the table)* You haven't touched your mail since Tuesday!

MATEY. Me and the Goddess has been talkin' confidential.

NANCY. *(Looking over the mail)* Perhaps it's in this lot—no. . . .

MATEY. It'll come Monday.

NANCY. Here's one from your broker, dated May 24th. . . .

MATEY. A circular, probably. *(He takes the mail from* NANCY, *slitting the envelopes with his scalpel.)*

NANCY. Oh, I meant to ask you,—are these of any use? *(She takes two square slips of paper from the pocket of her apron.)* They were in the pocket of that smock you wanted washed. *(Giving him one of them, she studies the other.)* They're not sketches, are they? I had one fearful moment when I thought you'd gone in for cubism.

MATEY. Not I! This is merely a demonstration proving that if a National Advertising Campaign increased our sales—I mean Warren's sales—only four per cent, it would more than pay for itself.

NANCY. *(Dryly)* What could be fairer than that? *(Proffering the second bit of paper)* And this—?

MATEY. *(More reluctantly)* It's a diagram showing that by running the raw mix from the vats direct to the ripeners by pipe, we'd save at least two and one-half per cent on our production costs. . . .

NANCY. Most ingenious of you. I suppose I'd best reserve a separate drawer for these. *(She holds out her hand for them.* MATEY *stares at them dumbly for a moment, then tears them up and jams the pieces into his pocket.)*

MATEY. Habit again! Must I ride two horses my whole life long?

NANCY. *(Calmly)* That, I presume, is the question. (MATEY *begins to read his mail.)*

MATEY. Remind me to pay my insurance policy Tuesday, will you? Here's another notice from them. And the infernal income-tax on the fifteenth. Otherwise, they'll double it. Hope the dividend's not late. . . . (NANCY *takes a bill from his hands.)*

NANCY. Here—I'll take that. It's a bill for Jean's mumps.—Whew! They've gone up—fifty dollars a mump!

MATEY. *(Giving her another)* What do you want done about this?

NANCY. *(Which she returns promptly)* Nothing. By now those Armenians must be living on caviar.

MATEY. *(Reading a letter)* Good Lord!

NANCY. What's the matter?

MATEY. *(As he goes to the sofa)* Is this a morning paper?

NANCY. "The Times." Dear—what *is* it? *(She reads the letter which* MATEY *extends to her.)* Oh, how awful. . . . (MATEY *opens the newspaper to the financial page.)*

MATEY. It may have been a false alarm. I don't see anything. Yes—here it is—— Here it is, all right—and worse than they prophesied, too.

NANCY. *(In spite of herself)* If you'd only got this letter in time!

MATEY. *(Ironically)* Ah, no!—I was too busy with my brushes, to watch the market, and read my mail. *(He scans the letter again.)* Well—I've got to have cash by Tuesday, loss or no loss. You'd better take Hubbard's advice, and hold on to your stock. I'll go to town and see him right away. A fine mess I've got us into!—Matey and his money—they were soon parted, weren't they?

NANCY. *(Her comforting arms about him)* Dear

—*don't* say things bitterly, like that. We didn't expect this to be a bed of roses. . . .

(Up from the stairs comes RICKY, *gold-trousers—linen coat—homespun, and over one ear a troubadour cap, with flowing feather. He has a guitar tied around his neck by two long silk stockings, and thrums a chord as he enters.)*

RICKY. Say, Nanny—where's the rest of my costu—— *(He discovers his parents once more unmindful of their dignity.)* Will you two *never* grow up? (NANCY *and* MATEY *part, looking a little sheepish, and* MATEY *goes to a chair at the window—reading the paper.)* I feel more like Chanticleer than a troubadour. Don't mind my freezing on to a pair of your stockings, do you? Lord! You must have long legs!

NANCY. *(Primly)* I mind very much. There's a ribbon with the rest of it downstairs.

RICKY. I cannot relinquish the socks. *(He crosses to* MATEY, *thrumming and singing)* "List to me, Lady Love, heark to my plea——" *(But stops suddenly at the sight of* MATEY'S *face.)* What's the matter, old Lad?—You look as though a mule had kicked you.

MATEY. *Two* mules, Rick——

NANCY. Your father has had bad news from his broker.

RICKY. *(All bantering aside)* Gosh, Dad—that's a rotten shame. I've got four hundred and sixty saved up, if that'll help any——

MATEY. The money for your wedding trip?

RICKY. *(Chamber of Commerce, please note)* What's Bermuda—compared to our own Niagara Falls?

MATEY. Thanks, Son—but I don't think I'll need

it. *(With an attempt at jocosity)* I may sell my picture over the week-end.

NANCY. It's finished. You haven't seen it yet. (RICKY *examines the portrait admiringly.)*

RICKY. I call this painting! Say, how about my buying it?

MATEY. You haven't enough.

RICKY. I'll take it on installments. Listen, lady— *(He prepares to sing to the picture)* "List to me, Lady Love——" *(But* MATEY *brings the serenade to a deservedly abrupt conclusion.)*

NANCY. What have you children been doing? (RICKY *finds a comfortable place on the window-seat.)*

RICKY. Ronny's had the nag out—went home to change—coming right over. I've been shooting clay pigeons—only got twelve out of twenty-five—but I gave the others a nasty scare. (NANCY *laughs.)* Say, Dad, G. T.'s up here with the Thompsons over Sunday. Said he might drop in to see you.

MATEY. I hope he does. Is he still handling most of my work?

RICKY. No—didn't I tell you? New man came in three weeks ago. Name's Chadwick——

MATEY. *(Sharply)* T. L. Chadwick—?

RICKY. Think so. He's famous as the Battle of the Marne—and acts it. They say he's dragging down forty-five thousand a year. He's taken over your job—*I* thought G. T.'d keep it open for a year, anyway.

(This has all been a considerable shock for MATEY. *For a moment he stares speechlessly at* RICKY, *then turns to* NANCY, *speaking in a changed voice.)*

MATEY. What time do you expect Geoff?

NANCY. About four-thirty.

MATEY. Good—I'll have time to see him before I leave. *(He goes out by stairs.* RICKY *rises, and with a gesture of disgust with himself, goes to a chair near* NANCY.)

NANCY. Rick—you must learn tact. You couldn't have chosen a worse moment to speak of that new man at Warren's.

RICKY. *(Shamefacedly)* I knew it as soon as I opened my face. I ought to be shot. But after all, Nancy, I can't say that I blame G. T. . . .

NANCY. *(Suddenly)* Are you really happy there?

RICKY. *(Off-hand)* Sure. Why not?

NANCY. Tell me honestly!

RICKY. *(Confidentially)* Well—you see it's this way: When I look at the men higher up in the office—men of about forty or so—and realize that if I barge through in really noble style that that's where *I'll* land at forty—I don't exactly jump up and down and clap my hands at the prospect. But after all—that's life, isn't it, darling?—You get some things, and some things you don't. And I've packed a *couple* of hearts full in Ronny and you—— *(To prove it, he kisses her cheek.)* You're a wench after my own heart.

NANCY. *(Persisting)* But *don't* you miss your architecture?

RICKY. *(Strumming)* Rarely think of it.

(RONNY *comes in, very fresh and sprightly, as the result of a ride, a tub and a pretty new dress.)*

RONNY. *(However)* I don't expect to sit down for several centuries.

RICKY. Serves you right for jumping that green mare. If I were her——

NANCY. "—if I were *she.*"

RICKY. *(A proper rebuke to the purist)* If I were her—I'd have bounced you off on your nose.

RONNY. *(So sweetly)* No, precious one—if you'd been the mare, I'd have taken you over the roof. *(She sees the portrait, which occasions a deep breath of admiration.)* Oh, this is too beautiful.

NANCY. *(Who is putting* MATEY's *paint table in order)* I'm inclined to agree with you, Ronny.

(But there is a sudden new interest, for RONNY *sees the mannikin. She picks it up and hugs it passionately.)*

RONNY. Oh—I want her! I want her!

RICKY. Name's "Genevieve." She's Dad's mistress.

NANCY. Ricky!

RICKY. *(With a gesture)* Art's his mistress. Genevieve is Art.

(RONNY *takes from a chair a piece of the same stuff as* ETTA's *dress, and wraps it about the figure's shoulders. Henceforward, "Genevieve" remains gratefully near her.)*

NANCY. *(As she moves toward the stairs)* I'll be back in a few minutes. If Mr. Nichols comes, you entertain him, will you?

RICKY. Certainly shall! (NANCY *goes out, and* RICKY *turns to his* RONNY.*)* As studios go—not so nasty—wot? *(He lights a cigarette for her and one for himself.)*

RONNY. I love it.

RICKY. Nanny calls it the Zoo. *(He takes her hand and conducts her across the room.)* Here you see a mountain-goat, at the age of seven months. And here—*(Indicating another specimen on the opposite wall)*—the same goat, several years later. (RONNY *nods gravely.* RICKY, *before letting her hand go, raises it to his lips and kisses it. For a*

"You and I"

Act I, See Page 29

silent moment life's infinite fulfillment looks out to each, from the other's eyes. RONNY *speaks softly.)*

RONNY. You dear—— *(But, after all, one must be practical.)* Not *very* stiff!—Chuck us a cushion, will you, Dreadful? (RICKY *procures a cushion from the window-seat and another from the sofa.)*

RICKY. *(Preparing a place for them on the floor)* Lord—three sets of tennis—and I'm fit for the ash-can! This working indoors all week takes it out of you, do you know it? *(They seat themselves, back to back on the cushions.)*

RONNY. *(Sleepily)* Um—— Now do you *really* like it there, Stupe?

RICKY. Child, I'm engrossed!

RONNY. Sure?

RICKY. Absolutely! I'd no idea soap and tooth-paste could hand me such a thrill. Had a talk with G. T. this morning. Told me I'd rate three thousand as soon's I marched back down the aisle.

RONNY. He's a sweet old thing. We'll be filthy rich. *(Yawns.)* Umph!

RICKY. I regard that as a deliberately unfriendly act.

RONNY. I'm a dead bunny.

RICKY. Not too sprightly myself. . . Let's play shut-eye for a while.

RONNY. *(Closing her eyes)* You're on. Night-O. . . .

RICKY. *(Hunching his shoulders)* Move over.

RONNY. Great Oaf! *(They close their eyes, and there is a short pause.)*

RICKY. ". . . and God bless everybody in this house." *(Another short pause.)*

RONNY. —Two minds without a single thought. *(—And still another. Then* RONNY *begins to wriggle.)* Hell's bells—I'm being prodded in the spine. What is it?—something in your pocket, or just—anatomy . . .? (RICKY *is wide-awake in a moment.)*

RICKY. *(Eagerly)* Oh—I forgot. *(Rising, he puts out his cigarette, and extracting an old book from his pocket, again seats himself.)* Look here, Beau'ful—I picked this up in a bookstore this noon. Sixteen dollars. It's a first edition of Mossgrave's "Architecture, and ye Associated Artes"—published in 1611—illustrated with woodcuts—rare as hell.

RONNY. *(Regarding it sleepily)* Priceless!

RICKY. You said it. And look—— *(He opens the book to the flyleaf and proudly points to the signature thereon.)*

RONNY. "I. Jones—His Book."—Should I be impressed?

RICKY. *(Ironically)* A little. Do you know who it is?

RONNY. I bite: Who?

RICKY. *(Impressively)* This book belonged to—Inigo Jones!

RONNY. What a screaming name. *(To "Genevieve")* Did you hear that, Genevieve?—"In-again Jones." *(To* RICKY*)* She wants to know who he was?

RICKY. *(Witheringly)* Just one of the greatest architects that ever lived, that's all. Designed Whitehall, and Queen's House, and a few miserable little things like that. Not *very* famous.

RONNY. *(Somewhat abashed)* I am the Indian Club among Dumbells.

RICKY. *(Studying the pages)* And look at this—isn't it great? *(He becomes engrossed in the book.* RONNY *watches him closely.)* Honestly if I could design a façade like that, I'd die happy—and this gargoyle—you see the vine-motif has been carried—

RONNY. *(Quietly)* Put your arm around me, Ricky. *(Absently he does so.)*

RICKY. *(Going right on)* The vine-motif has

been carried out even here. And I'll be blowed—this must be one of the very earliest developments of the rose window——

RONNY. *(Experimentally)* Rick—I want to be kissed—— (RICKY *kisses her. A piece of paper falls from the book to the floor.* RONNY *sighs.)* Oh—that's rather delightful. . . .

RICKY. *(For the moment, genuinely moved)* Damn right! *(But only for the moment, for he turns back to the book, almost immediately.)* The facing shows that it's at a very primitive stage——

RONNY. *(A certain heart-breaking realization is slowly tightening about her)* Does it . . . ?

RICKY. Um. . . . *(He sees that she has picked up the piece of paper and is studying it listlessly.)* Here—lay off! That's not finished yet!

RONNY. What is it?

RICKY. It's a plan I was making for our new diggings. Now you know what made me late for your dinner last night. (RONNY'S *face lights up; here is hope.)*

RONNY. *(Eagerly—handing it to him)* Tell me about it!

RICKY. *(Explaining)* You see—I wanted something we could add on to—the way Dad and Nancy did to this. First comes the cellar—for the furnace and things. Downstairs: hall, living-room, dining-room—that little hole is the library, kitchen—out back, servants' quarters above it. Upstairs: four bedrooms—yours and mine, and two guests' rooms. Three baths. Top floor: small store-room and play-room. . . .

RONNY. For us . . . ?

RICKY. *(Solemnly)* For our progeny.

RONNY. Isn't it big! How many do you think there ought to be?

RICKY. Oh—conservatively—three or four. . . .

RONNY. *(Thoughtfully)* Well—I'll see what I

can do. . . . *(She leans over to examine the plans more closely.)* What are these?

RICKY. *(With additional enthusiasm)* Ah—here's the real work! Look, Beau'ful—the stables—miniature reproduction of Charles the Second's at Windsor. And this is the kennels—just like some I once saw for St. Bernards at a monastery near St. Moritz.

RONNY. *(Regarding him oddly)* They're more interesting than the house, aren't they?

RICKY. Ever so much! You see it's one of my pet convictions that you can make any building beautiful—even a cow-shed,—without in the least contradicting its original charac—— *(He regards her in surprise.)* Dearest! What is the matter with you? You look like the very devil——

RONNY. *(Confused)* I—? Why— I— Don't be a fool, Rick— *(Her hand brushes across her eyes. She sighs, shakes her head, and laughs shortly.)* I'm—just simply in a fog over tonight. . . . *(*RICKY *regards her dubiously, then becomes matter-of-fact once more.)*

RICKY. Oh, say—I don't want to muff that troubadour stunt. Slip me the dope again, will you . . . ?

RONNY. *(Lifelessly)* It's—not my idea, you know. It's Mother's: We're to have supper on the south terrace at twelve. When they're all seated, you amble up below the second story window, and begin—— *(*RICKY *begins thrumming and singing gayly. As he does so,* RONNY *frowns over the revelatory little slip of paper.)*

RICKY. *(Singing and strumming)*

"List to me, Lady Love, hark to my plea:
Love holdeth no bounty so precious as thee,
Flown my heart's gayety, lovelorn my life,
Sad and desolate I, save I have thee to wife."

—and then you press a red, red rose to your lips,

and toss it lightly to me, and I catch it in my teeth, or something, and *voila!*—— *(He strikes a chord)* The kitty is out of the bag!

RONNY. *(Slowly)* And suppose—instead—I just —turned away—and shut the window—*would* you be sad and desolate—?

RICKY. On the contrary, I should execute a few choice clog steps and sing:

"Be she fairer than the day
Or the flow'ry meads in May—
What care I how fair she be
If she be not so to me?"

(During the song RONNY *has rolled the plans together into a small roll.)*

RONNY. *(Rising)* Is that the way you'd really feel—do you think?

RICKY. *(Gayly)* Sure!

RONNY. *(Quietly)* I'm glad.—Because I—don't——

RICKY. Don't what . . . ? *(His soft strumming continues, an ominous accompaniment to the words that follow.)*

RONNY. Don't love you, Rick. *(The mannikin is permitted to topple to the floor.* RICKY *looks at* RONNY, *appalled—and then laughs.)*

RICKY. *(Scoffing)* No—that's why you're marrying me!

RONNY. It's—why I'm *not.* . . . .

RICKY. *(Not to be taken in)* Too late now.

RONNY. It's—just this side of—too late. . . . *(Pause.* RICKY *is trying bravely to smile.)* I—*mean* it, you know.

RICKY. *(With difficulty; his smile comes and goes—he stands the guitar against a chair and goes to her)* Ronny—please find some other way to—

ride me. I'm—you're—I—you see, I'm such a fool about you that I can't—play up to this.

RONNY. *(Speaking in a small voice)* It—breaks me into little pieces—but I mean it. *(He takes her hand.)*

RICKY. *(Dazed and incredulous)* Ronny—you —you simply *can't*. . . . (RONNY *withdraws her hand.)*

RONNY. Do—you remember that day last Autumn—what I told you about Father and Mother? (RICKY *tries to speak, but nods, instead.)* How I said I was going to marry the next nice person I was—fond of? You were the nice person, Ricky— *(Shakes her head, sorrowfully.)* Oh—the nicest one! And I thought surely I'd love you. But—I don't. And I can't—just *can't* go through with it, without——

RICKY. *(With effort)* I—don't know what to do. I don't know what's expected of me. I—don't quite understand it. Nearly—but not quite. I can't believe that you—you've simply got to tell me some more about it. . . . *(There is a sound at the stairs.* RICKY *glances over his shoulders. His voice lowers)* Hell—Nichols, I suppose. . . . The playroom —quick! *(He holds the playroom door open and follows her through, closing it after them.)*

(ETTA *comes up the stairs, dressed as a lady still, but carrying a sobering dust-cloth. She places the guitar upon a trunk and begins aimlessly to dust. Goes to the portrait, looks at it adoringly, turns about, as though posing before a mirror, the better to see her profile, then suddenly pirouettes to her first position. She picks up "Genevieve," and looking about to see that she is alone, places her upon a chair facing the dais. Then, draping herself in the throne-chair, she touches her hair lightly with the arched tips of her fingers, assumes a rather weary expression, and begins to talk to her inanimate companion.)*

ETTA. *(Affectedly)* Yes—*such* weather! Just *too* dreadful! I've had no gulf for weeks. . . . *(Lowly, to herself)* Gulf—golf—galf—gowf—guff—— *(This satisfies her. Aloud)* I have had no guff for weeks. *(A pause. Then she smiles, and extends a properly limp hand to the air.)* Oh—ah—how-do-you-do?—So good of you to come. *(She waits for the inaudible answer.) No!* What a piddy! *(Lowly, to herself)* Piddy—pity—pitt-ty—*(This is quite satisfactory, so she tries it aloud) What* a pitt-ty! *(Pause. To "Genevieve")* But my deah—my bridge is *simply* deplorable! *(Pause. This has been a good one, and she is well pleased with herself. There is more than one person at this most de luxe of receptions, so she greets another)* Oh—ah—how-do-you-do? *(The response is audible this time, for* GEOFFREY NICHOLS *has quietly mounted the stairs to the studio.)*

NICHOLS. How do you do? (ETTA *has one very bad moment, but fortunately regains composure in time.)*

ETTA. *(What's good for one is good for another)* So—good of you to come——

NICHOLS. *(A little surprised)* Thanks. Permit me to present myself: I am Geoffrey Nichols.

ETTA. *(This with effort)* How do you do? I am—Miss—Henrietta Hone—— *(With a gracious gesture)* Won't you sit down?

NICHOLS. Thanks—— *(He finds "Genevieve," however, the occupant of the logical chair. Tenderly he places her upon the floor, and takes her place, facing* ETTA.) An extraordinary person at the door told me that Mrs. White would be up here——

ETTA. Oh, yes—that was Katie. What a piddy—*(Oh! She has muffed it!)*

NICHOLS. Not at all! I consider myself very fortunate. Are you staying with the Whites?

ETTA. Yes.

NICHOLS. Charming, aren't they?

ETTA. *(A little less securely)* Yes. *(Pause.* NICHOLS *is rather taken aback by her apparent aloofness.)*

NICHOLS. *(At a loss)* Er—— (ETTA *turns quickly.)*

ETTA. My deah—my bridge is *simply* deplorable.

NICHOLS. *(Sympathetically)* I'm *so* sorry. Mine is, too. Will they expect us to play? (ETTA *looks away, not answering.)* I hope not. I've just gone two rounds of goff, and——

ETTA. Of *what* . . . ?

NICHOLS. Of goff—and lost six balls, and most of my mind. (ETTA, *unnoticed by him, forms the word "goff" several times with her lips.)* I've been chanting the "Götterdämmerung," with variations, most of the afternoon—— *(It is not a distaste for Wagner that causes* ETTA *to flinch.)*

ETTA. Mr. Nichols—I do not consider such language at all refined.

(For one appalled moment, NICHOLS *stares at her. Then he realizes that she is, of course, purposely burlesquing. This guest of the Whites' has, indeed, both originality and charm! He laughs delightedly.)*

NICHOLS. Delicious! *(He settles himself more comfortably, and speaks with amused gravity)* Of course, I ain't exactly what you'd call a *gent*—but I gotta hearta gold. . . . (ETTA *never changes expression.)* How long have you been here with the Whites?

ETTA. Oh—quite awhile——

NICHOLS. I must take Nancy to task for this. I'm a native now, you know. I've taken the Burton place for the Summer. I can't think why I haven't seen you. . . .

ETTA. Do you attend the dances at the Odd Fellows Hall?

NICHOLS. *(Not to be outdone)* No—I'm of the Loyal Order of Moose. But I hear they're real tasty affairs.

ETTA. *(Soulfully)* They are grand.

NICHOLS. *(We are getting on)* What a delightful person you are! Won't you lunch with me tomorrow?

ETTA. *(Slowly)* Why—I *can't*——

NICHOLS. Then when *may* I see you?

ETTA. *(Hesitatingly)* Uh—uh—Thursday afternoon?

NICHOLS. Splendid! We'll motor out to Waukubuc.

ETTA. That would be elegant.

NICHOLS. *(Mockingly)* "Excuse our dust!" *(A silence; he finds nothing to top that mental image of a red and white pennant on the back of his car.)* Do you suppose Nancy knows I'm here? (ETTA, *who has had enough practice for the present, rises and goes quickly to the stairs.)*

ETTA. I'll go tell her. . . .

NICHOLS. *(Protesting)* Oh, please—I didn't mean—I'm enjoying myself so much, really. . . .

(ETTA *continues straight on, regardless. At the top of the stairs, she meets, coming up,* NANCY, *who has changed to an afternoon dress.)*

NANCY. *(Hastily to* ETTA) The flowers for tonight have come. Bring them up here now. And you must change—*at once!* (ETTA *goes out.)* Geoffrey—do forgive me. I simply had to scrub up.

Did you just arrive? *(She moves toward portrait.)* Look! The *chef d'œuvre* is finished! Now please tell me honestly what you think of it. Isn't it enchanting? Would you believe my Matey could do it?

(NICHOLS *is more than a little puzzled. He glances toward the stairs and proceeds to play safe.)*

NICHOLS. *(Enthusiastically)* Such grace of line! What a flair for color! The flesh tints are exquisite. It's simply incredible!

NANCY. Yes. . . . There—we've done our duty! Now tell me what you *really* think. (NICHOLS *permits himself the steadying influence of a cigarette.)*

NICHOLS. Well—upon my word, I don't know. It's such an extraordinary fine likeness, I suspect it's not great work. He may be merely—clever with a brush—as I'm clever with a typewriter.

NANCY. *(Feelingly)* Oh—I *hope* it's not that! *(Realizes what she has said, and laughs.)* Geoffrey —you know what I mean——

NICHOLS. No—I am completely mashed. *(They seat themselves upon the sofa.)*

NANCY. *(In a business-like manner)* Our really pressing problem now is how to sell it.

NICHOLS. *(Reflectively)* If I only had a stationary home——

NANCY. That's very kind. But he wouldn't hear of it, anyway. How *does* one market pictures—do you know?

NICHOLS. Why—I suppose you get them exhibited. . . .

NANCY. You've a nice broad back. Will you walk up and down Fifth Avenue?

NICHOLS. That *was* helpful, wasn't it?

NANCY. If only someone would want it at once.

NICHOLS. Has he done anything else?

NANCY. Just a few sketches. It was difficult, getting under way.

NICHOLS. Such a different life—quite natural. Last Autumn, I did my best to dissuade him. Frankly—how do you think he likes it?

NANCY. Oh, underneath, I think he's been very—I think he's been *happier*——

NICHOLS. Good! You know, apart from my personal interest—to me Matey is Everyman.

NANCY. How do you mean, precisely?

NICHOLS. My gardener kept me occupied for twenty minutes this morning telling me what a splendid carpenter he would have made—and means to make still. *(He laughs shortly.)* He's sixty-three.

NANCY. *(Thoughtfully)* I see. But is it the same?

NICHOLS. Maybe not.—How have you weathered the change?

NANCY. I've tried—oh, I've tried so hard! *(With a little shudder.)* It's shameful the way prosperity softens one.

NICHOLS. *(Incredulously)* You—?

NANCY. *(Nodding)* It's a little pathetic, you know, to find you're the sort of person whose conception of a real sacrifice consists in managing with two servants, instead of five.

NICHOLS. *(Nothing truer, you know)* Nonsense! Sacrifice is relative. You suffer as much from lack of luxuries as another woman from lack of meat.

NANCY. Maybe—but it's rather disconcerting to reach down into your—depths, and touch bottom so quickly.

NICHOLS. Matey's not faltering, is he?

NANCY. *(Rising)* No—only a trifle worried. The family budget does it—it's not precisely bulging. And today—poor dear—he's had such upsetting news—*(With a wry smile)*—Someone at a directors' table said, "Please pass the dividends."

NICHOLS. What a bore. *(Thoughtfully)* I wonder if I couldn't——

NANCY. *(With a grateful smile)* No—he wouldn't let you. When it comes to taking help, he's the rankest of egotists!

NICHOLS. But—— *(A thoughtful pause. He rises and looks at the portrait. His face lights up.)* Nancy—I've an idea! This portrait—it's really charming. Now Mrs. Carhart is having her usual drove of twenty or so up for the week-end. There are certain to be a few wealthy patrons of art among them, and——

NANCY. *(Excitedly)* Geoffrey!

NICHOLS. I'm sure that if I asked her, she'd hang it in her drawing room. One of them might want to buy it. At any rate, they'd talk—and it would be a fair test of its worth. The only difficulty is, that if they damned it, Matey would be so cast down that——

NANCY. You darling! Listen: he won't have to know anything about it! He's going into town on the four-fifty-one—coming out again later in the evening. . . .

NICHOLS. Yes?

NANCY. Yes.—Can't we take it over right after he goes—and have it back before nine-thirty? They'd have plenty of time to see it. . . .

NICHOLS. I don't know why not. But—if it wasn't a go, some one of them might speak about it afterwards. . . .

NANCY. But they won't know who did it! You see—it isn't signed! Say it's the work of an unknown painter—a protégé of Matey's—just in case —*(Turns to portrait.)* Oh, it isn't dry yet. Suppose we had an accident with it?

NICHOLS. That's not likely—wrap it carefully. I'll drive over now and see her—come back for you about five-thirty. Then we'll—— *(There is a sound on the stairs.* NANCY *murmurs, "Sh-h-h!" and nods an excited assent.* MATEY *enters.)*

MATEY. What's to happen at five-thirty? I shan't be here.

NICHOLS. That's just the point. Nancy and I are going to run away together.

MATEY. Good! She needs a change. *(He indicates the portrait)* Have you seen the—uh—"White" . . . ?

NICHOLS. Rather!—I'm delighted with it.

MATEY. Isn't he nice, Nanny?

NANCY. No one has ever so endeared himself to me.

MATEY. I'm going to let the Metropolitan and the Luxembourg fight it out. Look here, Balzac—what do you think of this left arm?

NICHOLS. But my good Gainsborough—I find it a bit muscular!

MATEY. That, my dear Hawthorne, is light—not muscle.

NICHOLS. But I tell you, Sargent, that I know a muscle when I see one!

MATEY. The thing I want really to know, Chambers, is just how well *do* you see?

NICHOLS. Quite well enough, Mr. Christy, to know a tendon from a sunbeam.

MATEY. Harold Bell, I find you a very stuffy person. . . .

NICHOLS. Oh, Briggs!—Think what you'll suffer when the critics start to bark! (MATEY *throws up his hands in surrender.* NICHOLS *becomes serious.)* By the way, Matey—I've five or ten thousand that's simply mouldering away. Do you know of any trustworthy individual who'd be willing to take it on for a year or so at, say, six per cent . . . ?

MATEY. Why—— *(He looks suspiciously at* NANCY, *who brazens it out.)* There must be any number of them, old son. But I can't think of one just at the moment.

NICHOLS. If you hear of one, let me know. I'd consider it a favor.

MATEY. *(Slowly)* Yes—I'll let you know. . . .

NICHOLS. Well—I must be rolling along. The Duanes' dance ahead of me—and I haven't done a line all day.

MATEY. *(Amiably)* We artists must think of posterity, mustn't we?—See you later, anyway!

NICHOLS. Right-o. . . .

NANCY. I'll go down with you. . . . *(*NICHOLS *stands aside to let her pass, and is about to follow when* MATEY *stops him.)*

MATEY. Oh—Geoff——

NICHOLS. Yes?

MATEY. Thanks very much—but I really think I can manage without it. . . .

NICHOLS. Without what?

MATEY. *(Smiling)* The five or ten thousand at six per cent.

NICHOLS. *(Impatiently)* *Damn* the interest, Matey.

MATEY. It's bully of you—but I don't think I'll need it.

NICHOLS. Well—in case you do—— *(He turns to go.* MATEY *goes to the far window and stands there, looking out. Just as* NICHOLS *reaches the stairs,* ETTA *comes in. She is in her simple gray working-dress once more, and carries a box of flowers and a water-filled vase.* NICHOLS *stares at her—his incredible suspicion confirmed.)*

ETTA. Good-by, Mr. Nichols——

NICHOLS. *(Genially)* Good-by. Oh—uh—if you don't mind, I'll bring my sister along with us Thursday. She's awfully nice—really awfully nice. *(With a gracious bow, he goes out.* ETTA *begins to ar-*

range the flowers in the vases. MATEY *comes over to the portrait.)*

MATEY. *(Absently)* What did Mr. Nichols say?

ETTA. I'm going riding in his auto Thursday afternoon. It'll be wonderful practice. He's the funniest man!—I had a perfectly *lovely* talk with him before Mrs. White came in. (MATEY *looks at her in frank amazement. Then his brow puckers reminiscently, and he suddenly sees the joke on* NICHOLS. *He laughs silently to himself, but* ETTA *is aware of nothing amiss.)* I can't imagine how anyone *could* be much pleasanter'n Mr. Nichols.

MATEY. *(Genuinely)* Nor I! Friends are very nice things—and sons—and wives.—And money's a nice thing, too—you know that, when you haven't any. . . . (RICKY *enters from the playroom, looking very white and sick. He carries the roll of white paper—his "plans"—upon which he nervously twirls the engagement ring. At first* MATEY *does not see him.)* Job gone—income gone—Art's a hard mistress, Etta—she picks your bones dry——

ETTA. *(The champion)* Oh, *no,* Mr. White! Art is lovely—jest lovely.

MATEY. *(Seeing* RICKY) Hello, Rick!—Where did *you* blow from?

RICKY. Playroom. . . . *(There is a short pause.)* Father—you might as well know—it's all off between Ronny and me.

MATEY. *(Astounded)* What's this?

RICKY. *(With an attempt at a smile)* Over—done—*fini*—— We aren't going to be married.

MATEY. But I don't understand. . . .

RICKY. It took *me* a long while too. It was all—bogus. She wants to see you—don't know why. Please don't cross-examine her—I think I've asked about all the questions there are——

MATEY. *(Impotently)* But—tonight—?

RICKY. *(Turns to him)* Too late to call off the

dance, of course. We're going right ahead with it—just as if it were an—ordinary party. *(He laughs ironically.)* Not *very* different! *(He sees* ETTA, *who, you may be sure, is not missing a word.)* C'-mon, Etta—finish those later. (ETTA *goes out and* RICKY *turns again to* MATEY.) Be decent to her, won't you?—She's feeling pretty sunk.

(He picks up the guitar, but as he does so, a string twangs. With a scarcely perceptible shudder, he carefully replaces it upon the trunk. RONNY *appears in the playroom doorway. Her color is high, and her eyes very bright. She holds her chin up, as if by effort. For a moment their eyes meet, and* RICKY *contrives to smile, before he goes out, leaving her with* MATEY.)

RONNY. Mr. White——

MATEY. Yes, Ronny . . .

RONNY. Ricky—told you? (MATEY *nods, unable completely to hide his scorn for this little jilt.)*

MATEY. You don't love him, h'm—?

RONNY. *(Passionately)* Love him! Oh—if a year ago someone had told me that I'd ever love anyone as I love Rick now, I'd have—I'd have—— *(She cannot go on.)*

MATEY. Then I fail to see why you've——

RONNY. I'll tell you why!—If I told *him,* he'd just laugh me out of it. Give me your word no one else shall know—no one at all . . .

MATEY. *(After a pause)* Very well—my word.

RONNY. I'm between Ricky and the thing he wants to do. That's plain. If I don't marry him, he'll go abroad and study as he should. *(Her hand falls upon his arm.)* *You* know what it means to him. *You* know he *must* be what he's cut *out* to be!

MATEY. You dear child. . . . *(He picks up her*

hand and touches his lips to it. She takes it from him at once.)

RONNY. *(In pain)* Oh—please—that's Ricky's trick!

MATEY. You're very brave, Ronny, and very fine—*(She shakes her head violently)*—but we can't afford to send him abroad now. (RONNY *straightens up, puzzled and shocked.)*

RONNY. Wha-a-a-t . . . ?

MATEY. I am not a rich man. I depended largely upon my salary. It stopped when I left business.

RONNY. But you've *something*—and I only need half of what I have a year. Take the other half—put it with whatever *you* can. I'd be happier—*much.*

MATEY. My dear . . . But there's been bad news, you see. I've almost nothing, now—not even enough for Nancy and me.

RONNY. *(Cruelly)* Then why don't you go back to business? (MATEY *flinches, in spite of himself.)*

MATEY. One has—certain obligations to oneself—you know. (RONNY *squares off—a cold fury.)*

RONNY. I've just taken my heart and—*(With a gesture of breaking it between her hands)*—done *that* with it. For him—for my Ricky! And you can stand there talking about yourself! Aren't you his father? Aren't you responsible for him?

MATEY. *(Genuinely moved, but smiling a little)* You are telling me I've—given hostages to Fortune?

RONNY. *(Impatiently)* I don't know anything about "hostages." I just know that there's something big in Ricky, that's got to come out. You can help him—and because you *can,* you *must.* He's your son—you've let yourself in for it! *(This is too much.* MATEY'S *spirit is up at last.)*

MATEY. Listen to me: your reasoning's very bad. You say I'm responsible for Ricky. All right—I'm responsible for bringing him out of nowhere into a very lively, very interesting world—for giving him twenty-one years of every advantage a boy can have. Now why shouldn't I think of myself for awhile?

RONNY. When all that time you've been teaching him to love something, aren't you bound to stick by him till he shows what he can make of it?

MATEY. He had his chance.

RONNY. And now that it's gone, must he wait till he's—forty, or so—for another? *(This shot tells.)*

MATEY. *(Doggedly)* Why not?—That's what *I* did.

RONNY. So—you want everything to be for him —just as it's been for you——

MATEY. *(Sharply)* Please! Please!

RONNY. Only *you* had Mrs. White in its place. He'd have nothing: I'd feel like a thief. You're *used* to doing what you don't want to do. He's not. He'd be just—empty. . . .

MATEY. He can quit now, and do what he wants on his own.

RONNY. And so he would! But could he go abroad? Could he be all that he *might* be?

MATEY. That's up to him.

RONNY. It's up to——! Oh, we *can't* argue, can we? What makes my reasons right for me, is just what makes them wrong for you.

MATEY. That's the old and the young of it, Ronny.

RONNY. *(Swiftly)* But there's one thing we jibe on! Both of us love Ricky. What you won't do for duty, you *will* do for love!

MATEY. *(With a gesture toward his painting)* Do you know how I love this?

RONNY. Not half so much as Ricky! He's your *son.* He'll come first!

MATEY. *(Whimsically)* You haven't convinced me, Ronny. But you've reminded me that there's a very cruel law that rules most men's destinies.

RONNY. *(An avalanche)* Not only *men's! (She shuts her eyes in pain, swallows hard, shakes her hand as if to shake something out of it, and then raises her chin sharply.)*

(NANCY *appears at the top of the stairs, carrying a large piece of brown wrapping-paper and a ball of cord.)*

NANCY. Matey—your train. . . .

(RONNY *wheels about and confronts* NANCY. *For a moment you feel that she is about to attack her as she attacked* MATEY. *But when her voice is heard it is the voice of a broken-hearted little girl, trying her best to be spunky to the end.)*

RONNY. Doing anything special Monday morning?

NANCY. *(Puzzled)* Why, no.

RONNY. If I may, I want to come over—

NANCY. Do. . . .

RONNY. —and cry on your shoulder.

NANCY. But what has happened? (RONNY *flings her last words over her shoulder as she goes down the stairs.)*

RONNY. I'll be in about eleven! (NANCY, *bewildered, looks after her for a moment and then turns to* MATEY.) Matey—what *is* it?

MATEY. *(Grimly)* A joke on me—one of fate's funniest. *(He crosses toward the stairs, shaking his head and laughing softly and bitterly.)* Laugh, my dear—laugh at me. (NANCY *is gazing after him intently, as—)*

THE CURTAIN FALLS

ACT III

It is shortly after nine, the same evening, and the studio is unlighted, save for the bright moonlight which flows through the great dormer-window upon the empty easel. Through this window a string of Japanese lanterns is seen, glowing in the dim distance.

There is a sound at the stairs. NANCY *enters, and crosses quickly to the long table, fumbles for a match, scratches it, and begins to light the half-burned candles in the sconces.*

The increasing light shows that the fifteen chairs at the table have been hastily pulled back, and that the table has not yet been entirely cleared. The dappled-gray hobby-horse has been brought from its hiding-place, and upon it sits "Genevieve," a paper cap upon her head.

NANCY *is dressed as a Spanish lady. She wears a black dress, a lace mantilla of black shot through with jade green, earrings, beads, bracelets, and a jade comb in her hair, which is worn high, in the Spanish fashion.*

As she lights the candles, a heavy, halting step is heard upon the stairs. She seizes one of the sconces, and crossing to the stairway, holds it high above her head, to light the entrance.

NANCY. Geoff—do hurry. . . . *(Still the very slow, heavy steps continue.* NANCY *becomes impatient.)* Do you want him to come in and *find* us? *(The steps continue at the same speed.)* Be careful at the corner! *(A silence. Then the steps begin again, slower than before.* NANCY *is vexed.)* Oh—

I *know* you'll rip it to shreds! *(Pause. Then suddenly the steps begin to race.* NANCY *leaps back, and the tip of the portrait, wrapped in brown paper, appears, and behind it* NICHOLS, *who enters as if he had been hurled by a catapult. He wears a Pierrot costume of black and silver, a black skull-cap, and an enormous white ruff at his neck.)* Useless person—utterly. . . .

NICHOLS. Useless! Three flights of stairs without a mishap—and she calls me useless! *(Together they remove the paper and a protecting frame from the portrait, which* NICHOLS *replaces upon the easel.* NANCY *folds the paper, ties string around it, and conceals it and the frame.)*

NANCY. Do you really think there's a chance? (NICHOLS *extracts a watch with great difficulty from somewhere within his clothes.)*

NICHOLS. Mrs. Carhart sent word that she'd 'phone me here before nine-thirty. *(He looks at the watch.)* Sixteen past. By a lightning calculation, fourteen minutes left.

NANCY. *(Seating herself at the table)* I wonder who it could be.

NICHOLS. *I* haven't the slightest idea.

NANCY. But whom was she having up?

NICHOLS. She expected the Graysons, and the Hoyts——

NANCY. Wait a minute! *(She takes down the names, writing with a crayon upon a piece of* MATEY'S *sketching-paper.)*

NICHOLS. And the Crams, and Reggie de Courcy——

NANCY. Wretched little worm. Tony Cram must be blind.

NICHOLS. And the Webbs, and Gregory Kendall——

NANCY. It might be Kendall! Wouldn't that be luck?

NICHOLS. Doubt if it's Greg. He once dined with Whistler. And the Warrens——

NANCY. The G. T.'s—?

NICHOLS. Yes—not staying there. Just came in with some other people for dinner.

NANCY. Well—we can cross *them* out. Go on.

NICHOLS. And Mrs.—what's her name—Parkerson——

NANCY. The front-page Parkerson?

NICHOLS. Herself.

NANCY. *(With a grimace)* Me-aow! Who else?

NICHOLS. Burke McAllister, and the David Ewings. . . .

NANCY. Precious, fat old things! *They* might—

NICHOLS. It'd be a great feather for Matey if he made their November Loan Exhibition.

NANCY. They're the ones!—It's come to me in a vision!—That all—?

NICHOLS. So far as I remember.

NANCY. Perhaps three or four of them will simply battle for it. You referee, Geoff—*(Thoughtfully)*—and perhaps no one will want it at all. And what will my Matey do then, poor thing . . . ? *(Dropping her head upon her hand.)* Oh—I'm too old to be as excited as this over anything! What *can* be keeping him? *(She goes to the window and looks out.)* See the lanterns strung through the orchard at the Duanes'. They look like plums and oranges, come suddenly to life. . . . Ricky—the lamb—he was such a corker at dinner. Kept them in perfect gales of laughter—just as if nothing had happened at all. Oh—that wretched girl.

NICHOLS. Odd—her tacking about this way, at the last minute. Simple funk, perhaps. . . .

NANCY. Nonsense! She dives twenty feet, without turning a hair!

NICHOLS. I could dive forty—before I could marry.

NANCY. What time is it now?—Come here—let's go over this again—— (NICHOLS *makes a movement to take out his watch. Then remembers what a task it is, and desists.)*

NICHOLS. *(Glibly)* Just nine twenty-one.

(MATEY *comes in.* NANCY *conceals the list.)*

NANCY. Hello, Matey. Thought you'd never come.

MATEY. So did I. That train was more than usually local. My dear—how charming you look.

NANCY. I am a product of Southern Spain, where men are men—and women, minxes.

NICHOLS. Three guesses what I am.

(ETTA *comes in.)*

ETTA. *(To* NICHOLS) There's a telephone call for you. (NANCY *starts, and then sets about concealing her excitement.)*

NICHOLS. Thank you, Etta. . . .

ETTA. *(Shyly)* You're welcome, Geoffrey. . . .

(NICHOLS *accelerates his exit, and* ETTA *turns to follow him.* NANCY, *with an effort, avoids the laughter that has overcome* MATEY, *and calls to her.)*

NANCY. Etta——

ETTA. *(Turning)* Yes, Ma'am——

NANCY. *(After a pause)* Ah—never mind. . . . (ETTA *goes out.* NANCY *and* MATEY *seat themselves upon the sofa.* MATEY *still laughs.)* I can't rebuke the girl. Matey—you *shouldn't* fool with people's souls, that way. She's miles above domestic service now. We must do something about her.

MATEY. *(Seriously)* Um. I know we must—

NANCY. It's a nice idea, though——

MATEY. What?

NANCY. That in creating the portrait of a lady, you may have created a lady as well. *(She glances toward the stairs and continues nervously)* How did you find things in town?

MATEY. Pretty bad. It took another slump today. I told Hubbard to sell four hundred shares at ten o'clock Monday. No use grousing over it, I suppose.

NANCY. Not the slightest. Let's forget it till we *have* to think——

MATEY. That's been our method with most disagreeable things, hasn't it?

NANCY. Um.

MATEY. And we've marched along pretty damn splendidly, haven't we?

NANCY. *(Nodding)* I'm so glad contentment hasn't caught us—and wrapped us in cotton-wool. We'll never be quite content, you and I.—So we'll never be dead until they shut our eyes and fold our hands.

MATEY. And even then I dare say our spirits will go on poking about the heavenly shrubbery—looking for birds that may be there!

NANCY. Darling—it's the way to live— *(Another furtive glance at the stairs.)* But it plays simple havoc with your nerves. . . . *(Suddenly)* Matey—tell me you love me.

MATEY. Child! I abominate you.

NANCY. Ah—very satisfactory.

MATEY. I particularly like you in earrings. (NANCY *taps one of the pendant earrings with her forefinger.)*

NANCY. "Waggle-waggle!" *(They laugh at their absurdity.)*

MATEY. I 'phoned Greg Kendall from the Club, but they said he was in the country. I've concluded that the thing to do with the portrait is to get an exhibition.

NANCY. *(Keeping her voice steady)* Kendall might even want it himself.

MATEY. I doubt it. But he often acts as an agent, you know.

NANCY. *(Airily)* Would you like Mr. Ewing to have it?

MATEY. Oh, no—not at all! Be hung along with Goya and El Greco? My dear—such ignominy! How did the supper go?

NANCY. Delightfully—for all but the three of us who knew. *(She shakes her head sadly.)* Ricky would have broken your heart.

MATEY. He didn't sulk?

NANCY. Matey!—Our boy *sulk?* He was splendid!

MATEY. I was certain of it.

NANCY. That girl! I don't see how she dares—

MATEY. Nanny—if only I could tell you.—Ronny—— *(He is interrupted by* NICHOLS' *entrance.* NANCY *goes to him quickly, and in the recess of the stairway they whisper together excitedly.)*

NICHOLS. Ssss-s-s-s—pss-sssh—pscpssch——

NANCY. Not *really!?*—But I never *heard* of anything so remarkable!

MATEY. *(Approaching them)* Here—what's this? Why not include the smaller nations in the conference?

NANCY. *(Motioning to him behind her back)* Go away! *(They whisper more earnestly.* MATEY *returns to the sofa.)*

MATEY. What *have* you two got up your sleeves?

NICHOLS. *(Over* NANCY'S *shoulder)* A white rabbit, now. It *was* a white elephant. (MATEY *picks up a magazine and begins to look it over.* NANCY *and* NICHOLS *join hands, and keeping perfect step, march over to a position in front of*

MATEY. MATEY *speaks to them indulgently.)* Yes, my little ones—what can I do for you?

NANCY. *(At once timid and exultant)* Maitland—Geoff and I have something to tell you. . . .

MATEY. *(Quite unimpressed)* Fancy that, now. (NANCY *turns imploringly to* NICHOLS.)

NANCY. I *won't* have my biggest moment ruined by such crass stupidity.

NICHOLS. Really, old son—we've three columns of news.

MATEY. Um.—Newspapers bore me.

NANCY. *(In desperation)* Matey—we've sold your picture.

NICHOLS. Not quite *sold,* but——

NANCY. At any rate, we've got an offer for it.

MATEY. Well, well—isn't that nice? *(He sighs.)* Come on—we might as well get it over with: Who has made the offer? (NANCY *appeals to* NICHOLS. *He laughs.)*

NICHOLS. The truth is that we don't *know* who!

MATEY. I shouldn't have spoiled it. Make it a good one: The—uh—Corcoran Gallery—or the Vatican—— *(Yawning and settling back.)* What tiresome people. . . . (NANCY *determinedly takes him by both ears, shakes his head, and literally lifts him to his feet.)* Here!—Let go!

NANCY. Matey! Will you listen? I tell you we're serious! (MATEY *looks at* NICHOLS, *who solemnly raises his right hand.)*

NICHOLS. By the bones of my ancestors! (MATEY, *dumbfounded, looks from one to the other.)*

MATEY. Well, of—— I'll be—— *Tell* me about it—quick!

NANCY. *(Eagerly)* It was Geoff's plan. He gets the credit.

NICHOLS. It was just as much yours as mine.

NANCY. But *Geoffrey*—you *know* you——

MATEY. *(Impatiently)* Honors are even! Come *on—what* . . . . ?

NANCY. *(Very rapidly)* Well—we took the portrait over to Mrs. Carhart's. Geoff had arranged with her to hang it in her drawing room, and show it to everyone before dinner—said it was by a protégé of yours. Then, just before you arrived, her chauffeur brought it back, and with it a message saying that she'd phone before nine-thirty. That was Geoff's call, and——

MATEY. *(Confused)* But—who—?

NICHOLS. That's what we don't know. It was her butler who 'phoned. Said she was sending the—prospective purchaser here to see me now.

NANCY. And it's probably either Kendall or the Ewings! They were both there. And it's an out-and-out offer——

NICHOLS. A handsome one, Matey—four thousand dollars.

MATEY. Four thousand dollars—for the work of an unknown modern?

NICHOLS. I made him repeat it three times. Not, of course, that I doubted its worth. . . .

MATEY. Oh, no—certainly not—of course not. But—*(In sudden buoyancy)*—I say! He must have *liked* it, h'm . . . ? *(He gathers* NANCY *to his side with one sweep of his arm, and grasps* NICHOLS' *hand.)* Oh—you bully good people! I wouldn't trade you for any other two on earth! *(He goes to the portrait.)* Geoff—bring those candles over, will you?

NANCY. No—let me! *(She picks up the sconce, and holds it up to light the portrait.* MATEY *dips his brush.)*

MATEY. Now for the great ceremony. Anonymity—farewell!

NANCY. *(Reluctantly)* I wonder if we aren't being a little—previous . . . ?

MATEY. *(With his brush poised)* Why . . . ? *(To* NICHOLS) Didn't you say it was definite?

NICHOLS. It seemed so to me.

NANCY. But—there might be a slip—'twixt the offer—and the check.

MATEY. *(Hesitating)* I wonder—— What do you think, Geoff?

NICHOLS. He'll be here in a moment. Why not wait?

MATEY. I bow to your good judgment. I'll sign it under his very nose.

NICHOLS. *(Suddenly)* I'm going to give up my popular writing, and see if I can't do one thing I'm not ashamed of——

MATEY. Fine! Of *course* you can. . . .

NICHOLS. I don't know. You jilted your art, but I did worse. I sent mine on the streets. She's not a forgiving lady.

MATEY. *(In high spirits)* Not forgiving?—When she came back to me after years of neglect? Try her! Try her! Now tell me: who else saw it?

NANCY. I have a list right here——

NICHOLS. I cling doggedly to a belief that it may be Mrs. Parkerson.

MATEY. I hear she has some beautiful things.

NICHOLS. And she likes new people.

NANCY. Matey—I *won't* let that woman have it!

MATEY. *(Good humoredly)* Not even for four thousand dollars?

NANCY. Not for twenty! (MATEY *draws a line and wafts a kiss to the dreadful woman.)*

MATEY. *Au 'voir,* Mrs. Parkerson. We thank you for your kindly interest—but our prig of a wife objects to you. *(He reads over the names.)* Of course—it might be any one of these—with two or three exceptions. . . .

NANCY. How I do hope that—— *(She hesitates,*

troubled.) It's almost too ideal to be altogether true.

MATEY. Nanny—you haven't been—pulling my leg?

NANCY. As if I could—in a thing like this! *(Again, apprehensively)* But—I mean—it seems so adventitious—so—pat to our needs.

(Enter RICKY *in a troubadour costume, but without the guitar.)*

MATEY. Still—if he definitely said—— Well, Rick, you look positively dashing.

RICKY. Keep your seats; the chorus will be right in. *(He sees "Genevieve" on the hobby-horse.)* I see the Lady Godiva still rides. Hi, Mr. Nichols!

NICHOLS. Hello, Ricky. *(To* MATEY*)* Don't you think I'd better go down and wait for—whoever it is?

NANCY. By all means. I'll go with you.

RICKY. Stick around a minute, will you, Nanny?

NANCY. I'll be with you presently, Geoff.

NICHOLS. *(Going out)* Right.

RICKY. *(To* NANCY*)* Ronny is downstairs. She wants to talk to you.

NANCY. I—don't think I care to see her now . . .

RICKY. Off that, Dearest. If Ronny wants to change her mind, why that's her privilege. I'll expect you to be just as nice to her as you possibly can be. And by that I don't mean any of your well-known politeness at ten below zero. . . .

MATEY. I haven't yet told you how sorry I am about this.

RICKY. *(Smiling)* Oh—it's not every one has *your* luck getting married.

NANCY. Come here, Rick—— *(He goes to her and she takes his face between her hands and kisses him.)* Tell Ronny to come up—— (RICKY *hugs her, drops his head upon her shoulder for a moment, and then looks up, smiling brightly.)*

RICKY. Thanks, old Precious—thanks. *(He goes out.)*

NANCY. Matey—he makes me ache all over.

MATEY. Our own good fortune seems nothing when I think of it.

NANCY. He'll get over it, of course—they always do. But a thing like this takes the sweetness out of a boy. It hardens him—makes him shrewd—metallic—— *(Exclaims in pain)* Oh—the poor darling! *(Flaming into anger against* RONNY.) And all along I've thought that Ronny's air of inconsequence was—merely an overlay—to many things fine, and true——

MATEY. My dear—it *is*——

NANCY. This looks it, doesn't it—this parody of love!

MATEY. It's hardly that, Nanny. And you must be very careful with her.

NANCY. *(Coldly)* And why should I be?

(RONNY *enters by the stairs. She wears a long dress of peacock-blue satin, brocaded with silver, a silver girdle and silver slippers. Binding her hair is a slim bandeau of pearls. It is the costume of a Seventeenth Century court. She looks considerably older—a charming woman of say twenty-six. She crosses a few steps from the top of the stairs, and stops.)*

MATEY. Van Dyck might have painted you.

RONNY. I wish he had. I'd like it better—if I were—just stuck up somewhere. . . . *(To* NANCY) I hadn't a chance at dinner—I wanted to be sure that—you weren't hating me too much——

NANCY. I'm afraid I am very old-fashioned.

Forgive me—but I find it difficult to regard jilting with anything but—distaste.

MATEY. *(An entreaty) Ronny—?*

RONNY. All right—only Ricky mustn't know.

MATEY. *(To* NANCY) Ronny told me something this afternoon—she told me a number of things. One of them was the motive for what she has done. She loves him very much. Rightly or wrongly, she felt that she was keeping him from the thing—from a perhaps notable career. So she broke her engagement, and gave him a trumped up reason for it.

NANCY. *(Incredulously) She* could do *that?!*— When I—? Oh— *(She stands with her head bowed, one hand resting upon the table.)*

MATEY. *(He must say something)* No doubt she's placed too much importance upon it. She's— (NANCY *turns to* RONNY.)

NANCY. Ronny—I think I am one of the few mothers who consider the girl their son loves really good enough for him.

RONNY. *(Barely audible)* You're very kind. But——

NANCY. *(With a gesture asking her to come to her)* Please—— (RONNY *crosses, and* NANCY *takes her hand.)* You make me feel very little. You are doing something that I, years ago, hadn't the courage to do. (RONNY *looks from her to* MATEY. *Then realizes what she means.)*

RONNY. Oh—it's not at all the same, you know.

NANCY. I think it is very much the same—— *(Pause.)* But—I don't know what to advise you. I've—had a happy life, my dear. . . .

MATEY. And so have I, Ronny—a very happy one. (NANCY *glances at him gratefully.)*

NANCY. It's—doubtful now, whether we *could* send Ricky abroad. . . . (RONNY *looks at* MATEY, *who looks away)* . . . even if he would consent to go. And it may be that you and your love could mean——

MATEY. Could mean—much more than anything else could, without them.

RONNY. *(Quietly)* As I see it, that's not the point——

MATEY. But the more I think of it, the more certain I am that——

RONNY. It's no good arguing, Mr. White. I'm sure I'm right. And you know what a stubborn little mule I am. . . .

NANCY. You've told your mother?

RONNY. That it was off? Yes. Told both of them. Father won't speak to me, and I left Mother eating aspirin tablets. *(She laughs shortly)* It's a great life.

NANCY. I only hope you're not making a mistake.

RONNY. It's not a mistake. Not if Ricky is started right. *(Again* MATEY *looks away.)*

NANCY. I'm afraid we couldn't afford—what do you think, Maitland? (RONNY *holds* MATEY'S *eyes for a long instant. Slowly he shifts his gaze to* NANCY.)

MATEY. *(With difficulty)* It—doesn't seem likely—no.

RONNY. *(After a pause)* Then at least he can go into an architect's office—you must insist on that.

NANCY. And perhaps turn out to be merely—clever with a ruler? No—he might better stay in business.

RONNY. Then—*(Almost breaking)* Oh—just because last Autumn I was a selfish, short-sighted little fool, is this all to be useless now? *(She looks at* MATEY, *and after a moment he turns and meets her gaze without flinching.)*

MATEY. One thing's certain: If Ricky is to do it at all, he must have the best training possible.

"You and I"

See Page 31

RONNY. *(With a wan, grateful smile)* I knew you'd think that.

MATEY. *(After a short pause)* Happily, I've just had some rather good news about—my painting. And——

RONNY. Oh—I'm *so* glad! (MATEY *smiles his thanks.)*

MATEY. And it is possible that the success of this particular piece may make my future work even more profitable.

RONNY. *(Her eyes shining)* Then—everything's all right for *both* of you, isn't it?

MATEY. That's what I'm hoping. So I think you may be confident that your very fine and generous sacrif——

RONNY. *(Swiftly)* Please don't say "sacrifice." It's not one—not if Ricky comes through as I know he will.

MATEY. At any rate, what you have done will not —go for nothing.

RONNY. *(Lowly)* That's good of you. Thanks. I'm—satisfied now. *(She turns.)* I'd better go back —the people have started to dribble in.

MATEY. Will you tell Ricky I should like to see him here in about half an hour?

RONNY. *(Lifelessly)* I'll tell him. *(She begins to move toward the stairs. Reaching* NANCY, *she turns impulsively, and buries her head in her shoulder.)* And I thought love all just a happy lark!

NANCY. *(Tenderly, as she pats her head)* Not all, dear. (RONNY *smiles much as* RICKY *did and straightens up quickly.)*

RONNY. Not—*any*—— *(There is a sound from the stairs and* WARREN'S *voice is heard.)*

WARREN. *(With difficulty)* *Is* there any top? Or—do we—just—keep going——?

NICHOLS. *(Cheerily)* Push on, Brave Heart—push on!

MATEY. *(Lowly, to* NANCY*)* Lord—I forgot Rick said G. T. was up here. I'll take him downstairs. Geoff should have known. *(He quickly moves the easel back into the shadow, and covers the paint table with a silk scarf, which he snatches from a chair. The sound draws closer, and* RONNY *steps back to let* WARREN *and* NICHOLS *enter.* WARREN *wears a dinner-coat, and looks quite exhausted.)* Hello, G. T. I heard you were somewhere in the neighborhood. *(They shake hands, blocking* RONNY'S *exit.)*

WARREN. *(Breathlessly)* H'lo—White—— *(He looks around for a chair, and finding none near by, sits upon a trunk.)* I'd—no idea—your house—was so tall.

NANCY. How do you do, Mr. Warren? So long since we've had this pleasure.

WARREN. How-do-do, Mrs. White. I expected—Saint Peter.

MATEY. I think we'd be more comfortable downstairs.

WARREN. Maybe we would. But—now that—I'm up—here—*(Taking a deep breath)*—I'm going—to sit down—long enough—to—make it pay. *(He sees* RONNY, *and rises.)*

RONNY. How do you do? (WARREN *looks puzzled at first, then beams and shakes hands with her.)*

WARREN. Why—bless my soul—it's Miss—Miss Duane, isn't it? My, how pretty you look—just like a picture. Your young man is doing very well for me. I—uh—understand the secret's coming out tonight. Let me be among the first to congratulate you—he's a fine boy.

RONNY. *(Glancing furtively at the stairs)* Thank you very much.

MATEY. *(To save the situation)* G. T.——

WARREN. *(Going right on)* Yes, a wife's the

best thing in the world for a young man, if he can afford one—*(He chuckles)*—and I'll see to it that *you* two don't starve right away. *(And continues talking to her, while looking at* MATEY. RONNY *quietly slips out.)* Expect big things of Ricky. Don't doubt that some day he'll be more valuable to me than his father ever thought of being. And I once thought White indispensable! Well—I mustn't keep you too long. I wish you every happiness—*(Turning about slowly)*—my dear. And I'm sure—*(He sees that she is not there, and laughs.)* Humph —that's one on me!

MATEY. G. T.—there are two or three things I'd like to mull over with you. Let's go down to the library. We can talk better there. I'm expecting a caller—but he won't keep me long.

(WARREN *goes to the sofa,* MATEY *watching him anxiously.* NICHOLS *goes to the window and stands there silently looking out, weaving his fingers in and out behind him.)*

WARREN. Don't see anything wrong with this. *(He seats himself and his long pent-up curiosity finally breaks through)* White—what on earth've you been doing with yourself?

MATEY. Oh—resting—and indulging a few neglected tastes. (WARREN *looks to* NANCY *for corroboration.)*

NANCY. You said he needed a rest, you know.

WARREN. Eight months of it? It's not resting after the first six weeks. It's rotting. . . . Well, I'm not here to talk vacations.

(NANCY'S *hand flies to her mouth. She bites her knuckle, drops her hand, turns quickly and looks at* NICHOLS. *He crosses to them.)*

NICHOLS. Oh, yes—Mr. Warren saw the portrait, Matey—— *(Dance music begins to be heard faintly, from the Duanes'.)*

MATEY. *(Easily)* That's right—you were at the Carharts', weren't you? Amusing chap—this protégé of mine. A bit erratic, of course—you know painters. . . .

WARREN. Um.

MATEY. Oh—by the way—did you hear Ewing or Kendall say anything about coming over?

WARREN. Here?—No. And listen—those fellows make me tired. You should have heard them pulling your friend's picture to pieces. All about "dim cherry-askuro" and "flat composition"—and all that high-brow rot. Blind as bats—both of 'em! Missing the greatest thing about it! *(Leaning forward, and tapping* MATEY'S *knee confidentially with his forefinger)* White—I want to tell you that that picture has Human Interest Appeal!

MATEY. *(Bravely)* You—found it interesting?

WARREN. *(Settling back)* Enough to pay four thousand dollars for it!

NANCY. *(Quietly)* You—are the prospective purchaser, Mr. Warren? (NICHOLS *returns to the window.* MATEY *nods his head reflectively, staring at the floor.)*

MATEY. H'm—very generous offer, very——

WARREN. You bet I am!—Why, it's the sweetest face I ever saw! *(He rises and crosses to the easel.)* This it? Ah—if that doesn't give trumps to all the Old Masters *I've* ever seen—— *(He gazes at the portrait with a rapt expression.* MATEY *brings himself heavily to his feet.* NANCY *edges closer to him, watching him.)*

MATEY. You say—Kendall and Ewing and the others—didn't think so much of it? (NANCY *is at his side.)*

WARREN. *(Snorting)* Bah—they make me sick!

MATEY. *(Very softly)* They make *me*—a little sick. . . . (NANCY *grasps his hand behind his back, and presses it as tightly as she can, as* WARREN *moves the easel around to get the full light upon the face.)*

WARREN. But that didn't change *my* opinion. If you discovered this, I'm tremendously indebted to you.

MATEY. *(Dully)* Oh—not at all——

WARREN. But I tell you it's just what I've been after for years! It's the most perfect type you could ask for!

MATEY. Type—? Perfect—? What *for—?*

WARREN. *(Triumphantly)* Why—to personify the Warren Line, of course!

NANCY. Oh—this is unthinkable!

(WARREN *looks at her, surprised. He has not caught the words, but the tone was unmistakable.* MATEY *drops his hand upon her shoulder, removing it in an instant.)*

MATEY. Just a minute, dear. *(To* WARREN) Let me get this straight.—Precisely why is it that you want the picture?

WARREN. Advertising, man, advertising.—What did you think? (MATEY'S *head sinks.)*

MATEY. I—*didn't*——

WARREN. Why—you ought to be delighted. Haven't you been howling for years for a big national campaign? And haven't I been holding out till I could find a way of putting the whole line over as a unit? Well, your dream's coming true,—'n so's mine—— *(Tapping the shoulder of the portrait.)* And we owe it all to this lady right here.

MATEY. Ah—this is Fame!

WARREN. You're right it is!

NICHOLS. *(To* MATEY*)* Millais once did a painting for Pears' Soap, you know. . . .

MATEY. Thanks, Geoff.

WARREN. Look!—Can't you just *see* it with "The Warren Line is Purity Itself" written in nine-point script across the bottom?

MATEY. Instead of the painter's signature. Yes—I can see it. *(He turns and regards* WARREN *speculatively.)* G. T.—you're not aware of it—but in a way you're—uncannily like God.

(NANCY'S *head drops upon her breast.* NICHOLS *abruptly returns to the window. The music at the Duanes' stops, and the faint sound of laughter is heard.)*

WARREN. *(After a pause. Surprised, then amused)* Me—? God—? Ho! Ho!—Thanks for the compliment. *(Again contemplating the picture)* Wonder if it wouldn't be better to put something in her hand. Art Department could retouch it in—a bunch of flowers . . . or a can of talcum——

NANCY. *(Quietly)* I think, Mr. Warren, that its great charm is its—refreshing freedom from artifice——

WARREN. Well—you ought to know. You're a woman—and it's women we want to reach. *(To* MATEY*)* Make the check out to you?

MATEY. You'd better wait. The—artist may not care to have it used for advertising purposes. I'll—let you know Monday. . . .

WARREN. *(Laughing)* What? Temperament? *(He goes to the table and writes a check.)* Wave this under his nose. If he's as poor as most artists, he'll soon forget his highty-tighty notions.—And tell him I want to see him about doing two or three more, in different poses. Same price. . . .

MATEY. *(Directly)* That I am certain he will not consent to.

NANCY. *(Softly)* Ah—you *brick!*

NICHOLS. *(Simultaneously)* Bravo!

WARREN. *(To* NANCY) What's that?

NANCY. I was speaking to my husband.

WARREN. Oh. (ETTA *enters with a note for* MATEY. WARREN *leaves the check on the table, and rises.)* You watch—he'll come around. He'll—

MATEY. It is—the *face* you like, isn't it?

WARREN. Certainly. I don't know anything about the technique, or whatever you call it. (ETTA *passes* WARREN, *unnoticed by him.)*

MATEY. I think perhaps we—can find the model —and some proficient—commercial artist can do her in other poses.

WARREN. Suits me.—Say, now—before I go— there's one more thing——

ETTA. *(Giving* MATEY *the envelope)* A message for you, sir—and thank you, sir.

MATEY. *(Gravely)* All right, Etta. (ETTA *joyfully turns to go out.)*

WARREN. *(Continuing)* I'm not too well pleased with the way the Chicago—— *(As she passes* WARREN, ETTA *looks up at him. He stops speaking abruptly, and his mouth drops open in amazement. He turns and watches her as she goes out. He looks again at the portrait, then wheels about quickly, and explodes.)* White—there's something damn queer about this whole thing. Did *you* paint this picture?

MATEY. *(Smiling)* G. T.!—Imagine me an artist!

WARREN. *(Suddenly his face lights up in complete understanding) Now* I see it! *That's* why you left! You knew we had to advertise! You knew I couldn't find what I wanted. So you got a big idea—worked it out by yourself—and then sprang it on me! What a fellow you are!

MATEY. It's a pretty explanation,—but quite erroneous, quite——

NICHOLS. Oh, agree with him, Matey—what's the odds?

MATEY. You're quite wrong——

WARREN. Dammit, right *or* wrong, I want you back. And now that I've O.K.'d your advertising plans, you ought to be on hand to manage 'em.—Well, what do you say?

MATEY. I don't know. I'll—tell you that on Monday, too. *(Thoughtfully)* If I should come back—would you agree to my having Fridays and Saturdays free the entire year round—to devote to a—hobby of mine?

WARREN. Absolutely!

MATEY. I'll think it over, and let you know.

WARREN. *(Tapping the portrait)* Have this sent to me, will you?

MATEY. If the artist agrees. Your house?

WARREN. No—right to the office. And you ought to shake up that Chicago crowd, and shake 'em up good! You could leave Wednesday and be back by the first of the week. . . .

MATEY. *(Reflectively)* I'd have a lot to tell those fellows.

WARREN. I bet you would!

NANCY. *(Alarmed)* But didn't you say that week-ends were to be free?

WARREN. Oh, occasionally it may be necessary to—— *(With a gesture.)* Business is business, you know.

NANCY. *(Softly)* So it is. . . .

WARREN. Well—I'll be going along. Good-night, Mrs. White.

NANCY. Good-night.

WARREN. *(To MATEY)* Expect to hear from you Monday. No need to come down with me.

NICHOLS. *(Crossing from window)* No—let

me—— *(As he passes* MATEY, *he stops and looks at him searchingly.)*

WARREN. *(On the stairs)* Good-bye! Good-bye, Mr.—uh—uh—*Good*-bye! *(He goes out.)*

MATEY. *(With a smile)* No, Geoff—not done yet!

NICHOLS. It's a rotten shame—*I* know what it's like—— *(He follows* WARREN *down the stairs.* MATEY *tears open the envelope and extracts the note.* NANCY *crosses to him.)*

MATEY. Something of a facer, isn't it?

NANCY. Oh, Matey—be careful, be careful! Don't do anything till you're sure that you're right.

MATEY. No, dear. . . . *(Turning to the signature of the note.)* H'm—from Greg Kendall——

NANCY. *(Eagerly)* Oh—what does he say? *(*MATEY *frowns over the writing.)*

MATEY. "Ewing and I—home—a lovely—" *(He gives it to her.)* Can you make it out?

NANCY. *(Reading slowly)* "Ewing and I have had a lively discussion concerning the portrait painted by your protégé. Ewing insists that——" *(She stops and looks at him fearfully.)*

MATEY. *(Grimly)* Let's have it.

NANCY. "Ewing insists that it is of no consesuence, but I cannot bring myself wholly to agree with him. . . ." *(Delightedly)* Matey!

MATEY. Crumbs are good.

NANCY. *(Continuing)* "I find the technique above average, and the brush-work distinctly promising. My main objections hang upon a certain inflexibility in treatment. We do not expect a painter's early work to be individual, but such rigidity is as ominous as it is uncommon. *(She turns the page.)* . . . Unless your young friend is content with a place in the ranks of the agreeably mediocre, he should devote the next three or four years to the most painstaking study under a good European master. This may, or may not, be his salvation."

MATEY. *(Staring straight in front of him)* And there's not a better judge than Kendall!

NANCY. No . . . ?

MATEY. Nor a fairer one. But it doesn't convince me—do you understand? Not by half! Ah—how I'd like to show them!

NANCY. You will—I'm sure you will.

MATEY. *(Grasping at the straw)* He did like my brushwork. You see?—That's very important.—Now if I should get someone in town to tutor me—

NANCY. You—who have just said, "If he's to do it at all, he must have the best training possible"—? *(He looks at her oddly.)*

MATEY. *(Half to himself)* Which of us——

NANCY. You're not one to do things by halves. Why not go abroad, as Kendall advises? *I* shan't mind—and it's no one else's business. Rick can support himself. I've still enough for Jean and me. And—*(She hesitates)*—for *you*—why, we can sell the place, you know. It ought to bring enough—land's valuable up here.

MATEY. But Nanny—you love it so.

NANCY. So do I—love you.

MATEY. But it's yours—it's your own——

NANCY. *(Softly)* Have I—anything—my *own?* . . . (MATEY *draws her to him.)*

MATEY. Ah—my dear—— *(A pause.)* I don't know what to do. I don't know. This afternoon—I'll never admit that all Ronny said was right. But on one thing we were agreed—on a weakness of mine—— *(There is a tinge of harshness in his forced gayety.)* A *weakness,* Nanny—that's what love is, in an artist! *(From the stairs comes the sound of whistling.)*

NANCY. What was it she said?

(Ricky *comes in, softly continuing the tune the orchestra at the Duanes' has been playing.)*

Matey. *(With a gesture toward him)* This—

Ricky. I am informed, O King, that you command my presence. Let the royal tongue wag— *(He sits on a trunk and begins to whistle again, low.* Matey *looks at him speculatively)*—or, in the vulgar parlance, shoot—

Matey. Ricky—how do you feel?

Ricky. *(With a short laugh)* Well, Dad, if you really want to know, I feel like holy hell.

Matey. I thought so.

Ricky. But I promised to act like a little soldier. And when a fellow lets himself in for something, he's got to see it through, hasn't he? So— *(He whistles a bar.)* Cheero!—*(And goes on whistling moodily.)*

Matey. When—a fellow does *what?*

Ricky. Lets himself in for something—— *(He returns again to his whistling.* Matey *is in a study. Suddenly his brow clears, and he speaks spiritedly.)*

Matey. Rick, how'd you like to go abroad—as you planned? (Ricky *glances at him quickly.)*

Ricky. What? *(A thoughtful pause.)* Take the wherewithal from you? No—thanks a lot—but it can't be done. I'll manage all right in some New York office.

Nancy. That's the *you* in him speaking, Matey. (Matey *thinks rapidly for a moment.)*

Matey. But I've good news for you.—When you were born, your grandfather took out an endowment policy in your name. You're supposed to get it when you're thirty—a yearly income of about two thousand, for a term of five years.

Ricky. But—I'm only——

Matey. Hubbard's the executor. This afternoon

he told me that it can come to you now—provided I consider you old enough to expend it properly.

RICKY. Gosh, Dad—that's knockout news—

MATEY. And if you and Ronny are careful, it's enough to take her with you. Together, you'll have four thousand a year. You'll do better work than you would if you had more—

RICKY. But Ronny doesn't—

MATEY. Let me finish! Son—the happiness of a man's family can mean a lot to him—a tremendous lot. So if you've something you feel it's your destiny to do—something out of the beaten track—unusual—difficult—you'd better begin your married life doing it.

NANCY. *(Quietly)* And if you don't?

MATEY. The chances are it will never be done. (RICKY *looks from one to the other, bewildered.)*

RICKY. But listen—

NANCY. *(To* MATEY) Then what—? *(For a moment* MATEY'S *head sinks. He lifts it again, smiling.)*

MATEY. Why—then I suppose—you turn philosopher.

NANCY. Philosophy—to fill an empty heart. It must be rather dreadful. . . .

MATEY. . . . It *would* be—if one's heart *were* empty. But when it's full already—well—habit has a way of changing destinies, don't you think? *(He laughs lightly.)* How's that—for philosophy? (NANCY *turns away.)*

RICKY. Wait a minute, Dad—I'm in a perfect fog.—You're sure you don't need that money yourself?—It's yours, you know— (MATEY *shakes his head decisively.)* Then it—oh, it'd be—I mean, you simply couldn't beat it. Gosh, how I'd work— But as for Ronny— *(He looks up, smiling.)* She doesn't want me. . . .

MATEY. Tell her what I've told you—and see

what she says. (RICKY *looks at him searchingly.)*

RICKY. Dad—*what do you know?*

MATEY. *(With sudden sharpness)* Never mind what I know! Stop arguing, and try it—quickly—before your luck changes!

(RICKY *turns and starts for the stairs as fast as he can.* NANCY *picks up the guitar from the trunk.)*

NANCY. Ricky—! *(He stops, and she holds it out to him.)* Here— *(He comes back, and takes it.)*

RICKY. *(Breathlessly)* Thanks, dearest. . . . *(He kisses her hastily.)* I love you. . . . *(He makes the stairs in record time and goes out.)*

NANCY. His grandfather did nothing of the sort.

MATEY. I know he didn't. But he wouldn't have taken it from me—not for both of them.

NANCY. Are you certain—you're acting wisely?

MATEY. Wisdom has nothing to do with love, my dear.

NANCY. *(A stilled voice)* Matey—if this is a failure, it's a kind I've never seen before.

MATEY. *(Brightly)* Why—you talk as though I'd given it up entirely! Didn't you hear me arrange with G. T. for time to—

NANCY. *(With a hopeless gesture)* Week-ends . . . ?

MATEY. Um.—And by and by, when Ricky's on his feet, and Jean is married—— (NANCY *buries her head in his shoulder.)*

NANCY. *(Pitying him with her whole heart)* Oh —*Matey*—you'll be nearly fifty!

MATEY. You call that old!?

NANCY. *(Clinging to him)* I don't like the look of this—at all. . . . (MATEY *holds her to him, staring fixedly into space over her shoulder. The or-*

chestra at the Duanes' begins to play a waltz. His face brightens.)

MATEY. *(As briskly as he can)* Well—if we're going to the dance, I'd better get into costume. *(He blows out the candles, and* NANCY *turns out the lamps, leaving the room lighted only by the moonlight, which faintly illuminates the small windows, and flows strongly through the great dormer upon the portrait, and upon* NANCY. *A shaft of pale light lights the stairs from below.* MATEY *takes one last look at the portrait and then goes to* NANCY.) What hideous disguise have you got for me?

NANCY. The usual—a matador.

MATEY. No!—Tonight I shall be something different.

NANCY. But there isn't anything!

MATEY. Yes, there is— *(He picks up his smock and holds it out for her to see.)* I am going, my love —*(The smock envelops him now, and he turns to give* NANCY *the full picture as he stands there, a parody of himself and his hopes)*—as an artist!

(NANCY'S *hand goes out to him in a little vain protest. He takes the red Spanish berèt from the animal's head on the wall and sets it jauntily upon his own. He lifts "Genevieve" from the hobby horse, and takes* NANCY'S *arm through his. The three cross toward the stairs,* MATEY *with his head high—"Genevieve" on one arm,* NANCY *a tragic figure on the other—whistling the waltz with the orchestra, as—)*

THE CURTAIN FALLS

KEY TO BLUEPRINTS

Act I

1—Armchair
2—Gate-leg table
3—Armchairs—cane
4—Console Tables
5—Side Chairs
6—Sofas
7—Table with drawer
8—Waste Paper Basket
9—Bench
10—Antique Secretary
11—Mantel
12—Hearthstone
13—Fire Screen
14—Columns
15—Pilasters
16—Returns
17—Steps
18—Landings
19—Backings
20—Windows
21—Doors
22—Pipe for X-ray
23—Pipe for Baby Spots.
24—Open lamps
25—Baby Spots
26—Branch of tree
27—3 Birch trees
28—Balustrade

Act II

1—Italian Table
2—Sofa
3—Savanarola Chair
4—Easel
5—Work Table
6—Antique Trunk
7—Antique Chairs, large
8—High stool
9—Antique Chair, small
10—Throne Chair
11—Dais
12—Japanese Screen
13—Branch of Apple tree in bloom
14—2-Step.
15—Platform
16—Steps to Cellar
17—Bookcase
18—Newel Post, Balustrade
19—Baby Spots
20—Open Lamps on Stands
21—Open Lamps on Floor
22—Bear Rug

Act III

1—Italian Table
2—Sofa
3—High Stools
4—Side Chairs
5—Hobby Horse
6—Antique Chair, small
7—Bench
8—Savanarola Chair
9—Antique Chair, large
10—Trunk, antique
11—Easel

12—Work-table
13—Gate-leg table
14—Bookcase
15—Throne Chair
16—Dais
17—Stool
24—Japanese Screen.

AIR OF "COME O'ER THE SEA"

List to me, lady-love———hark to my plea!
- -0233 - - -022

Love holdeth no bounty so precious as thee:
- -0233 - - -022 - -0233 - - -022

Flown my heart's gaiety; lovelorn my life;
- -0233 - - -022

Sad and desolate I, save I have thee to wife!
- -0233 - - -022 - -0233 - -0233

TO THE TUNE OF "SHALL I, WASTING IN DESPAIR"

Be she fairer than the day,
- - -022 - -0234

Or the flow'ry mead in May,
- -4444 - - - -0- - -0- - - - -002

What care I how fair she be,
- - -2- - - - -2 - - -0 - - - - -2-1 - - - -1-0

If she be not fair to me?
- - -2- - - - -0- - - -4- - - - - - -022 - -0234

NOTE: The above fingering is *not* for the regular guitar tuning, but for special tuning, which is as follows:—

The string nearest the player to G and the others, in order, to C, D, G, B and D (the furthest string).

O indicates an open string to be played. The figures indicate frets. — indicates that a string is not to be struck.

Only the outer four strings are used in the above accompaniments.

PROPERTIES

A dark blue carpet covers the stage, stairs and landing.

A large table with drawer on the lower R. side stands up and down stage on R. just in front of door R.

A side chair is R. of it.

Large upholstered sofa is L. of the table, back to it.

Small bench with padded seat front of table.

Console table, half oval, stands up R. against the side flat in arch.

Large cane winged armchair stands obliquely between console and window up R.C.

Antique secretary desk between windows in back flat.

Small cane sofa is in front of window L.C. and near fireplace.

Mantel at fireplace with hearthstone.

Blue silk upholstered armchair stands just L. of C., back to audience, slightly turned toward the mantel and about two feet above the setting line of set. Marked armchair C.

A low antique gate-leg table L. of the armchair, the L. shelf raised. Marked table C.

Side chair, cane back, at corner below mantel, marked chair L.

Console table, half oval, stands in C. of piece at L.C.
Cane armchair is against the stairway, marked armchair L.
Piano off R. in solarium.
Blue silk cushions on window-seats in windows up R.C. and L.C.

SMALL PROPS.

On Table R.:
3 Magazines on lower R. corner.
2 Book-blocks and 8 books set obliquely at lower L. Writing-set at C. on R. with stationery, pens, pad, blotter, etc.
2 Glass ash-trays at corners on L.
Large lamp (Electric) in C. of upper end of table.
In Drawer on R. of table and lower end: Several free-hand sketches, typewriter-size paper and smaller.
1 Waste-paper basket above table.
1 small blue rug covers electric wire of lamp on T.C.

On Console table up R. against the side wall:
Large blue China vase filled with Laurel branches, with large orange-colored berries.
3 Books on lower end.
3 Magazines on upper end.

On Mantel:
2 large blue glass vases, flanged tops, with Laurel twigs in them, at either end of the mantel.
Glass ash-tray at lower end.
Wire screen at fireplace.

On Gate-legged table L. of armchair, marked T.C.
2 Magazines.
Silver smoking set.
Tray.

Ash-receiver.
Match-holder.
Cigarette box, filled.
On blue silk armchair, marked armchair C.:
Magazine on the seat.
On Console table at L.C.:
Lamp (Electric).
2 Small statuettes, one on either side of lamp—man and woman.
Small book.

PROPS. OFF STAGE

On Platform at head of stairs:
Half-written letter, stationery, matches that on table R.
Watteau print, about 12 x 14 inches, wrapped in tissue paper, then a nice store paper outside that, ends closed with stickers. The print is in a black frame, and glass.
Off L. 1st entrance:
Light-colored wicker tray, round and about 15 inches in diameter.
Silver cocktail shaker.
5 Cocktail glasses.
Napkins.
Back of window R.C.3: Birch saplings.
Back of window L. of C.: Branch of Birch Tree.

PERSONAL

RICKY:
Pipe.
Tobacco pouch.
Matches.
WARREN:
Pencil, Eversharp.
Piece of paper.

MATEY:

Pencil, Eversharp.

NICHOLS:

Watch.

HANGINGS

Pictures:

1 above console table L.C.
1 at L. of window L.C.
1 at R. of window R.C.
2 above the console table on R., one on either side.
1 large picture over mantel.

Curtains:

Window L. of C., 4 half-curtains, on rods, top and bottom, lace.
Chintz valance and sides.
Window R.C. Same as above.
Door down R. Lace, reaching from top to bottom on each half, on rods.
Windows in solarium: Three windows the same, Lace, on rods, reaches from top to bottom.
Cretonne valances and sides.

BRACKETS (Electric)

2 Arms, 1-10 Watt, round lamp, blue white, on each arm. Mirror sconce.
2 on wall above console table on L.C.
1 each side of the picture.
1 above the console table on R.

ELECTRIC EQUIPMENT

Foots:

12 to 15 lamps in each circuit, 60 Watts.
Frosted white, with a few drops of blue in it.

Moonlight blue.
Frosted pink.

X-Ray:

2-Sections, with Steel Blue. Flesh Pink, Amber, alternating. Blue medium in R. and L. of sections 6—150 Watt lamps in each section.

Battery Hanging Back Stage:

1000-Watt spots and open lamps numbered from L.

No. 1—White, open lamp, focused on window C., Act II.
No. 2—S-Blue, open lamp, focused on window L.C., Act I.
No 3—Spot, White, open lamp, focused on window L., and to hit the throne chair, Act II.
No. 4—Open Lamp, white, focused on window C., Act II.
No. 5—Open Lamp, S-Blue, focused on window R.C., Act I.
No. 6—Spot, St. Blue, focused on window R.C., Act I.

Baby Spots Hanging Front of X-Ray (Numbered from L.—250 *Watts):*

No. 1—Flesh Pink, focused on Sav. Chair, Act II.
No. 2—Flesh Pink, focused on Sofa, Act II.
No. 3—White, focused on Bear rug, Act II.
No. 4—White, focused on Matey at picture, Act II.
No. 5—Steel blue, focused on Throne chair, Act. II.
No. 6—White, focused on Throne chair, Act II.
No. 7—Flesh Pink, focused on Sofa, Act II.
No. 8—Flesh Pink, focused on Throne chair, Act II.
No. 9—Steel Blue, focused on Throne chair, Act II.
No. 10—Amber, light, focused on Matey at picture, Act II.

OTHER EQUIPMENT

4-2000 Watt baby spots on stands used on stage.

3-1000 Watt Open Lamps, on stands used on stage.
2-2 Lamp Strips for entrances:
 Steel Blue and Pink in one.
 Frosted White and Pink in other.
1-Tall Brass Table Lamp, Parchment shade, Acts II and III.
1-Shorter Brass table Lamp, silk shade, Act I.
1-Porcelain table lamp, silk shade, rectangular shape, Act I.
3 Wall Brackets, two armed and with one 10-Watt round lamp, frosted white with a drop of blue in it, on each arm.
Parchment shield shaped shades, and with Mirror Glass Sconces.

ACT I: LIGHTING

Electric Plot:
X-Ray — Up Full
Baby Spots — Up Full
Battery at back, No. 2, 5, 6 (Blues) — Up Full
3 Wall Brackets—Lighted
 (1 is above the console table up R. 2 are above the console table at L.C.)
1 Table lamp on table R.—Lighted.
1 Table lamp, Porcelain, on Console table L.C.—Lighted.

Off Stage, on R.:
 Open lamp, steel blue, through window.
 Open lamp, steel blue, above the window and straight down stage.
 Spot lamp, light pink and frost up stage and down through window.
 Spot lamp, light pink and frost, at upper corner of set and through window.

Spot lamp, light pink and frost, L. of window R.C. focused past the window.

Spot lamp, light pink and frost, at L. of window D. of C., focused past the window.

On Platform L.:

2 lamp strip, Frosted pink and white.

At Entrance on L.:

2 Lamp strip, Frosted blue and pink.

At Rise of Curtain Everything Is Up Full.

As Overture stops.
Take house lights slowly down and out on dimmer.

Foots: Bring in a very faint glow in foots.

As Curtain Rises:

Bring foots up to mark—

Blue	Up Full
Pink	Up Full
White	Up ⅛

CUES

As Nancy turns out lamp on table R.
Pull out—Pink and Amber circuits of X-Ray.
Pull out—Pink in foots.

As Nancy turns out lamp on console table L.C.
Pull out—blue circuit in X-ray.

As Nancy presses button above door on L.
Pull out—Baby spots, brackets, blue and white in Foots.

When Curtain is down come back with everything for the calls.

PROPERTIES

Act II

A brown linoleum covers the stage.

A Dais forty inches square and about ten inches high, covered with dull black oilcloth, is on R., just above the return.

Japanese screen, three pieces, stands back of the dais and the upper piece breaks on stage.

Large throne chair is on the dais, for the model.

In front of window R. is a large antique chair, Italian model.

In the upper corner R. is an L-shaped bookcase.

In the angle of the bookcase is a small antique chair.

At R. of window C. is a high stool.

At L. of window C. and partly in front of the balustrade is a large antique trunk.

Above door on L. large antique chair.

Below door on L. large Italian table.

At R. of the above a large sofa, with back to table.

At C. just above the setting line is a Savanarola chair facing the upper L. corner of set.

The easel is set up near the C. window so as to get the light; the left of it is on the C. line and it obliques toward the upper R. corner of set, so as not to show the portrait.

An artist's work-table stands at the R. of the easel.

SMALL PROPS.

On Italian table below door L.:

Tall wrought-iron candlesticks, tripod shape, and with a partly burned candle in each, stands at each end of the table (2).

Otter skin laid obliquely through C. of table.

Tall brass lamp, with parchment shade, stands in C. and on the skin.

Several magazines are on the L. of table between the candlestick and the lamp; two piles, one above the lamp, the other below it.

At the upper R. corner of table:

Four letters; one from the broker in large business envelope; others in different colored stationery, one of which contains a bill.

A glass cigarette box, filled.

Ash-tray and match-stand, combined.

On sofa, L.:

Newspaper, "The New York Times," at the lower end.

Large round cushion at the upper end.

On easel:

Portrait of Etta, on a sancas stretcher, no frame.

Several pieces of rags, for cleaning brushes, etc., on the shelf.

On work-table at R. of easel:

Piece of cardboard, rough edges, as though torn, about 10 x 5 inches, with "Fresh Paint" painted on it. A string, looped, attached, to hang over end of portrait. Upper end. Palette knife. Scalpel.

Several brushes of different sizes, upper end.

Three or four bottles, turpentine, etc., C.

Palette, upper R. corner.

Ash-tray, at lower L. corner.

Two large glass cups, for paint, C. lower end.

Three Porcelain cups, near lower end.

Tin dish, round, about 10 inches diameter, filled with tubes of paint.

Tubes of paint scattered about.

All of these articles show long usage and are covered with paint.

The upper L. corner of table has been used to mix the paint instead of the palette.

Artist's paint-box on shelf below table, tin.
On Throne Chair, used by the model:
Large silk shawl, pink color, is draped over back and arm of the down stage side.
On floor L. of Dais:
Large bear rug, black, head up stage and stretched obliquely down.
On antique chair in angle of Bookcase:
"Genevieve's" wooden lay-figure, about three feet tall.
On seat of window up C.:
On R. side a drawing-board leans against the side.
Portfolio filled with sketches next to it.
Artist's paint-box, wooden, on the portfolio.
Other sketches scattered about.
Cocoanut shell in C.
Red Spanish Beret next; large round pillow on L. matches on on sofa.
On balustrade:
Otter skin.
On bookcase, up in R. corner of set:
The top shelves are filled with books.
Bottom shelves with magazines, papers, etc.
On top of side on R.:
Two tall brass candlesticks and candles.
Small yellow bowl in which stands a glass cup, similar to the one on work-table, filled with sprigs of laurel, stands between the candlesticks.
On top of side facing front:
Blue Porcelain jug, on R.
Tall brass candlestick, C.
Large blue porcelain vase on L.
Outside window on R.:
Top branches of an apple tree, in full bloom, some of the twigs fixed so as to be easily detached.

Outside window up C.:

Top branch of a birch tree is seen in the lower L. hand corner.

HANGINGS

Pictures:

Large picture hangs on side wall above table.

Two smaller ones, on either side of the above and lower down.

Small picture at R. of window C., down low.

Plaster cast of man's head hangs at L. of window C.

The mounted head of a wild goat hangs in the alcove at head of stairs.

Another, skull and horns, hangs above the side of door on L.

Curtains:

At window C., tan colored, half curtains on rods, at top and bottom, four pieces.

Blue side draperies hang from the top to bottom, on rod.

At window on R., lace curtains on each half of window, on rods, from top to bottom.

PROPS. OFF STAGE

Below the Stairs:

2 small pieces of paper—Nancy.

1 with figures on it.

1 with a diagram drawn (see script).

Guitar—Ricky.

With two colored silk stockings tied to it, and looped so as to go over the head.

Old book on Architecture—Ricky.

Written on fly leaf of book—"I. Jones—His Book."

Piece of paper, 8 x 5, with diagram, as per script.

This book is about 7 x 4, goes in Ricky's pocket.

2 Dusting cloths—Nancy and Etta.
2 large flower boxes—Etta.
1 about 24 x 8 x 4, contains two bunches of spring flowers, also a single one for Nichols' buttonhole.
Other box, slightly longer, contains a bunch of Forcythia with long stems.
Flowers in both boxes nicely done up in waxed tissue paper.
2 blue glass flower vases (Act I)—Etta.
Personal: Engagement ring—Ronny.

ELECTRICAL PLOT

X-ray	Up full
Baby spots	Up full
Battery	Up full

At window on R.:
3 Baby spots.
1 white on apple blossoms.
2 steel blue on backing.

At window C.:
On R. open lamp, steel blue, half off, focused through window.
On L. open lamp, steel blue, half off, focused through window.
Spot lamp, white, focused through window to throne chair.
These lamps are all on high stands so the rays shoot down.

At entrance on L.—2 lamp strip.

At foot of stairs (below stage)—Bunch light.
12 lamps, 4 each of white, blue, amber.

As orchestra stops:
  Take house lights slowly out on dimmer.
  Bring Foots into a slight glow.

As curtain rises: Bring Foots up to mark:

Foots—Blue	Up full
Pink	Up ¾
White	Up ¾

Everything stands for the act.

ACT III

SCENE: The Studio. Same as Act II.

PROPERTIES: The large Italian table at L. has been moved to the C. Its R. side is in line with C. Savanarola chair is now above the table. Antique chair from bookcase at front. Rush bottom chair at lower L. Another at upper R. High blue steel at upper L. An Italian bench (similar to piano bench) at lower R.

The sofa has been moved back against wall at L. Work table is placed in front of window on R. Easel is moved to side of work table, obliqued so as not to show the portrait (which is removed). An old battered Hobbyhorse stands at the upper end of sofa with just room to pass between; head faces L. "Genevieve" is astride the horse. Gate leg table (Act I) has been brought upstairs and stands at R. window C. High blue stool at L. of easel. Small, low stool, at lower L. of Dais.

The Antique chair at window R. has been removed. Shawl on throne chair taken off. Bearskin removed. Pillows removed.

SMALL PROPERTIES: *On Italian table:*

Embroidered linen runners at each end and one down the center.

One of the Tripod candlesticks at upper end.

Large blue porcelain bowl below it, filled with flowers of Act II.

The ash-tray at upper L. of table.

Another tray at C. on R. The glass cigarette-box above the bowl. Some pieces of paper at lower end and pencils.

On gate-leg table at R. of window C.: Large lamp (Act II—Electric).

On seat of window C.: One of the Tripod Candlesticks.

On antique trunk, up L.C.: Matey's smock. The red Spanish beret.

PROPS. OFF STAGE: *Below stairs:*

Etta's portrait in a narrow black frame, a piece of compo-board the size of the frame and with a half-dozen pieces of cork stuck to it to protect the portrait; tied in a large piece of brown paper.

Small silver Salver.

Letter for Matey, written complete. (No stamp.)

Victrola: Fox trot record. Waltz record.

Cues:

1st—Nichols—Mr. Warren saw the portrait, Matey.

Commence fox trot.

Matey—uncannily like God.

Count four, stop fox trot.

2nd—Nancy—like the looks of this at all.

Start waltz.

Curtain—Stop waltz.

PERSONAL: Pocket checkbook, with perforated checks. —Warren.

Fountain pen. —Warren.
Watch. —Nichols.
Pipe and tobacco. —Nichols.

ELECTRIC PLOT:

The Studio is unlighted except for the bright moonlight which flows through the window C.

Off stage Lighting:

All lamps placed same as for Act II, and all with Steel Blue mediums.

In Battery:

Only lamps with Blue Mediums used, Nos. 2, 5, 6.

Below stage:

Bunch light is on to light the stairs.

On Stage:

The tall table lamp of Act II is placed on a small table R. of window C.

Everything inside the set is black.

As orchestra stops:

Take the House Lights down and out on dimmer.

No Foots on at Rise of Curtain.

Curtain rises on a dark stage.

Cues:

As Nancy lights the candle on table C. Throw in half of the Baby spots.

As Nancy lights the candle at window C. Throw in the rest of Baby spots.

As Nancy turns on the lamp at window C. Throw in the X-Ray—up full. Throw in the Foots—to mark. Throw in the Blue—¼ up.

Throw in the Pink—¼ up.

"You and I"

See Page 49

At end of Act:

As Nancy turns out the lamp at wi

Pull out X-Ray and foots.

When curtain is down come back with

for calls.

Don't throw in the *foots.*

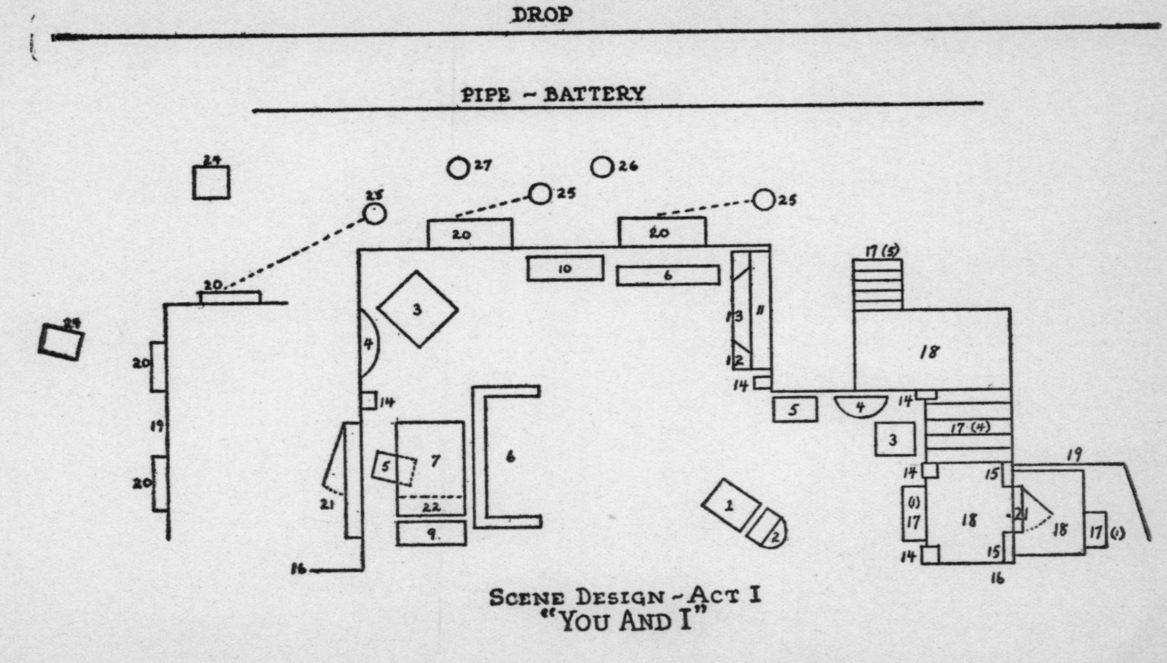

SCENE DESIGN - ACT I
"YOU AND I"

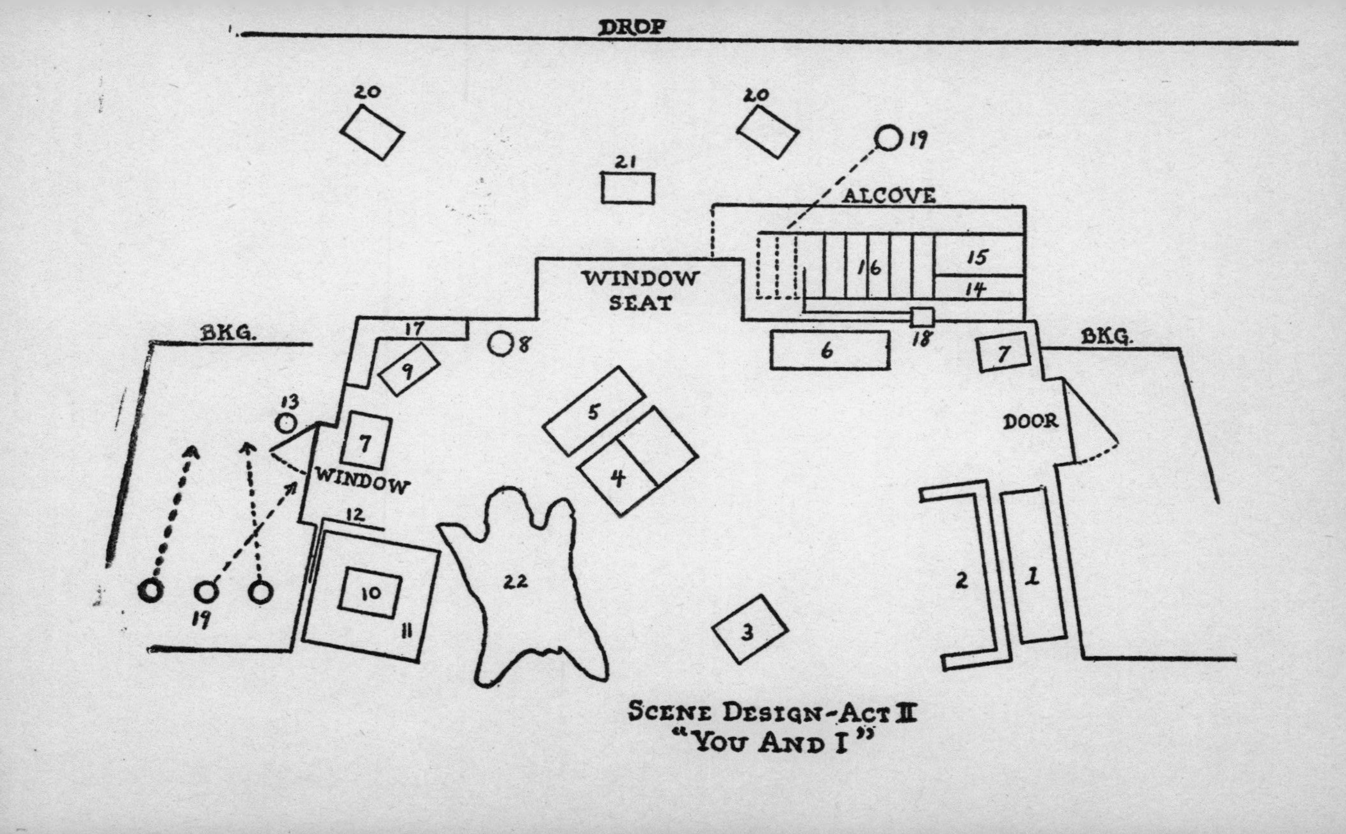

SCENE DESIGN-ACT II
"YOU AND I"

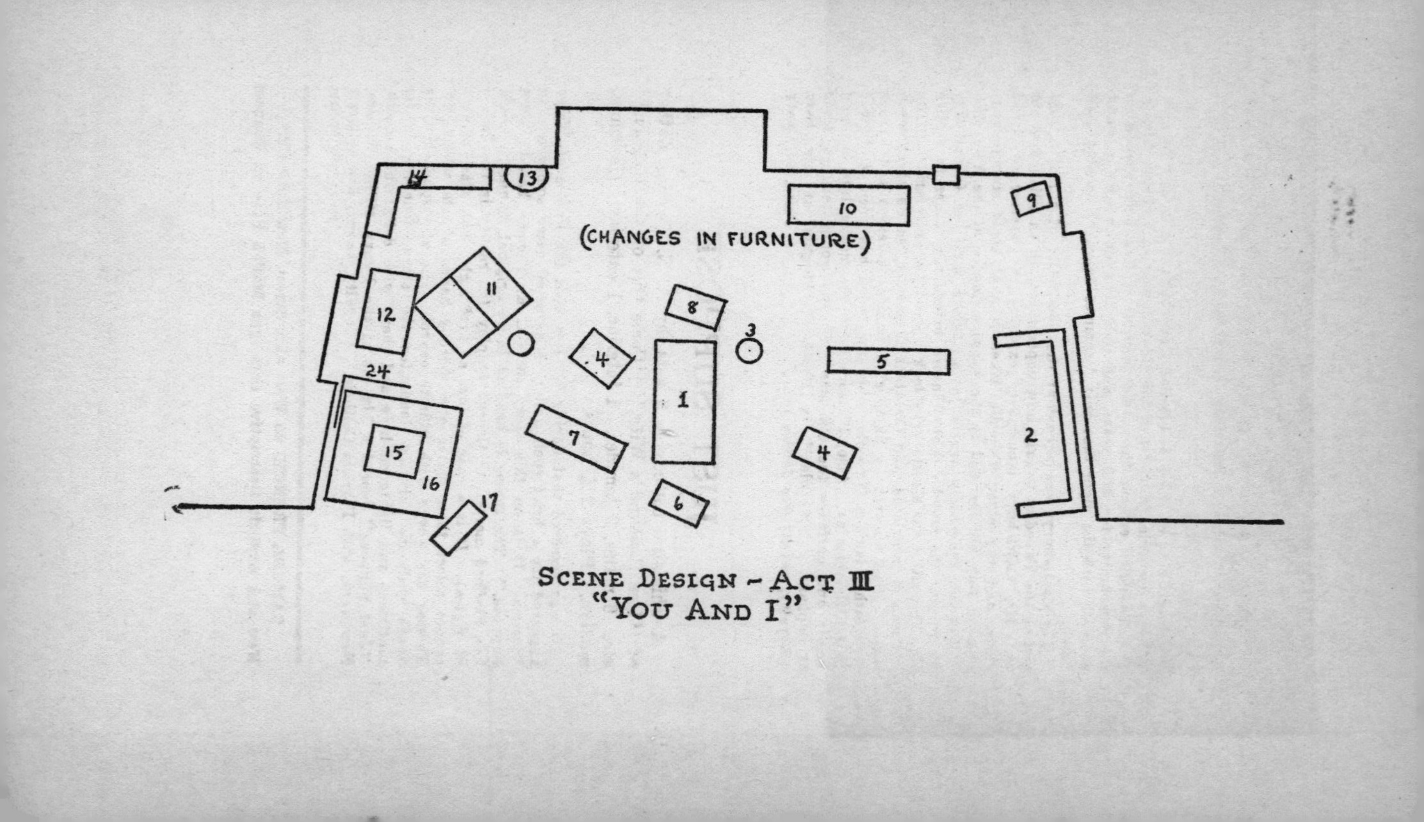

SCENE DESIGN - ACT III
"YOU AND I"